Johann Georg Zimmermann, Samuel Hull Wilcocke

Essay on National Pride

Johann Georg Zimmermann, Samuel Hull Wilcocke

Essay on National Pride

ISBN/EAN: 9783337005764

Printed in Europe, USA, Canada, Australia, Japan

Cover: Foto ©Thomas Meinert / pixelio.de

More available books at **www.hansebooks.com**

ACCOUNT

OF THE

LIFE AND WRITINGS

OF

Dr. J. G. ZIMMERMANN.

ACCOUNT

OF THE

LIFE AND WRITINGS

OF

Dr. J. G. ZIMMERMANN.

THE juſtly acquired celebrity of the author of the following Eſſay renders an account of his life a great deſideratum to the literary world. His renown has long been eſtabliſhed as a correct and energetic writer, a found philoſopher, and an able phyſician; and ſince, in his own words, (page 164,) " it is only for thoſe who lie mouldering in their graves, and who can no more be objects of jealouſy, to enjoy a reputation that envy cannot harm," now that he has paid his debt to nature, his memory will not fail to be revered by every man of genius, and his name handed down to poſterity with unfading honour.

John George Zimmermann was born at Brugg in the Canton of Berne on the 8th of December

1728.

1728. He was early deftined to the medical line and ftudied phyfic at the Univerfity of Gottingen, where he was a difciple and friend of the celebrated Haller. He firft refided and practifed phyfic at the place of his nativity, and afterwards at Berne,

We are not furnifhed with any particulars relative to him from this time till his removal to Hanover, except fuch as may relate to his writings. The lives of literary men indeed feldom abound with prominent features fufficient to arreft the attention; on which account, their biography is not unfrequently confined to the number and review of their works. Alike confcious of our deficiency, we muft alfo attempt to fupply it, as well as we are able, by giving a general information refpecting our author's writings; of which the following is a correct lift, in the order in which they appear to have been publifhed :

1. *Diſſertatio inauguralis de Irritabilitate.* 4to. *Gottingen,* 1751.

2. *The Life of Profeſſor Haller.* 8vo. *Zurich,* 1755.

3. *Thoughts on the Earthquake which was felt on the 9th of December* 1755, *in Switzerland.* 4to. 1756.

4. *The*

Befides thefe works we fhould mention his Effays in the Helvetic Journal, the acts of the phyfical and mathematical Helvetic Society, and thofe of the phyfiological Society at Zurich; and we likewife believe he publifhed a work on Zoology, of which we have not been able as yet to procure the title.

Moft

Moſt of theſe productions have been tranſlated both into French and Engliſh; and have proved equally acceptable acquiſitions to the phyſician, to the philoſopher, to the ſtateſman, and to the philanthropiſt.

Dr. Zimmermann therefore appears to have firſt diſplayed the dawnings of his great genius, which afterwards broke out with ſo much efful-gence, in a Latin Diſſertation on taking his de-gree of Doctor of Phyſic at Gottingen, and ſoon after by *the Life of Haller*, which was produced in the 27th year of his age. Though in the con-tracted ſphere of biography there was little ſcope for the poetic diction and forcible expreſſion which abound in his other writings, this Life of Haller prepared the expectations of the public, and announced the great talents which after-wards were ſo conſpicuous in the various pro-ductions which ſucceeded, and ſecured to him the applauſe both of his countrymen and of fo-reigners.

Of the beauty and excellence of the *Eſſay on Solitude* the Engliſh reader is already acquainted by the inimitable tranſlation which has quickly paſſed through five editions: this however being made from the French of Mercier, deviates in ſome inſtances from the German. In its original dreſs, dref, this performance runs through four octavo volumes; it is true there is much extraneous matter, and many parts that are folely interesting to Germans; nay fome that may be faid to be chiefly fo to the author's perfonal connections; but there are likewife other parts (although omitted by Mercier, from a mistaken regard to the illiberal prepoffessions of fome of his countrymen, and on account of the circumfpection and caution with which French authors were obliged to treat fubjects of a religious or a political nature) which to the liberal and uncontrouled fpirit of inquiry of Englishmen, would afford the higheft pleafure and intereft. Such for inftance are Zimmermann's confiderations on *Monaftic Solitude*, which extend nearly through two volumes, and which, fays the French tranflator, in his preface, " contain many profound reflections, yet are capable of difpleafing thofe whofe narrow prejudices might be fhocked by the liberal fentiments of an author, who appeals to the decifion of REASON alone upon the fubject of certain abufes, rendered facred by the motives from which they proceeded."

The great efteem which this work acquired on all fides was much enhanced by the grateful acknowledgment of one of the moft diftinguifhed perfonages of modern times. Dr. Zimmermann

was

was prefented in 1785 with a fmall cafket in the name of her Imperial Majefty the Emprefs of Ruffia. The cafket contained a ring enriched with diamonds of an extraordinary fize and luftre, and a gold medal bearing on one fide the portrait of the Emprefs, and on the other the date of the happy reformation of the Ruffian Empire. This prefent was accompanied by a note, written in the Emprefs's own hand, containing thefe memorable words: "To Dr. Zimmermann, counfellor of ftate, and phyfician to his Britannic Majefty, to thank him for the excellent precepts he has given to man-kind in his Treatife upon Solitude."

Of the *Effay on National Pride* we fhall fay but little, trufting that, in its prefent drefs, our readers may ftill admire the found reafoning and fund of entertainment it is univerfally allowed to poffefs in its original language. It was firft publifhed in 1758, and has gone through a number of editions.

The French tranflation of this valuable work is executed with elegance and precifion; with the exception in fome inftances of national partiality. It may be proper here to obferve, that the very great changes which have occurred in the politi-cal, and we may fay in the moral fyftem of Eu-rope, fince this Effay was compofed, will naturally conduce to make fome paffages lofe their effect,

and

and appear out of feafon; but the nature of man, which is the groundwork on which the author proceeds, remains always the fame, and we think we may affert with confidence, that whatever may be the apparent deviations from national character, and the feemingly contradictory appearances now obfervable in Europe, they will not only be found by the attentive obferver to be confiftent with the remarks and opinions of former times, but will, like muddy water fubfiding after a violent agitation, admit in the end the eye to pierce through the glaffy fuperficies, and behold the filth and corruption of the fediment.

A duodecimo volume, purporting to be a tranflation from the Effay on National Pride of Dr. Zimmermann, having been publifhed here in 1771, it may likewife be right to offer fome apology, for the attempt now made, to tranflate a work which has apparently already been produced in our own language. In extenuation of this feeming temerity, we beg leave to make public the following extract of a letter written by Dr. Zimmermann on the 27th May 1794 to Dr. Lettfom, relative to the above tranflation: " A pretended tranflation," Dr. Zimmermann thus expreffes himfelf, " of my Effay on National Pride has been publifhed in London, whereby the

the tranflator has rendered me nearly the fame fervice as if he had expofed my portrait, nay my perfon, in the pillory. If this pretended tranflator had only been ignorant of the Englifh language and of the art of writing, I could, on account of his good will, have pardoned him for the mifchief he did me : but he has fathered upon me a great number of puerile, flat, and trivial ideas of his own, which he has inferted in the text of my work ; this text he has crammed with Latin and Englifh verfe, a fingle line of which exifts not in the original ; and, notwithftanding what has been faid to my honour in the preface by a perfon of quite another ftamp, this pretended Englifh tranflator has made me appear like a fool throughout the work: fuch a tranflator is not only an ignorant fellow, but a cheat." Of the truth of thefe fevere animadverfions it would be unbecoming in us to decide. Thofe who will take the trouble to compare our tranflation with the original, will find, we hope throughout, a careful attention to exprefs the meaning of the author, and neither a modification or fuppreffion of any one fentiment, a liberty which we find, and have often had occafion to notice, in the French tranf-lator. In one or two inftances we have given our opinion in a note, which perhaps is the fole liberty allowable to tranflators.

The *Treatife on Experience in Phyfic* has not only been found an ufeful book to the faculty, but being cloathed in a novel elegance of language, fuch as the fubject was fuppofed not capable of admitting, has alfo readily found its way into other hands, and has conduced to the inftruction and amufement of the fofter fex. It has recently been objected, that this work did not contain any new difcoveries or theories, but we ought to carry our thoughts and opinions at leaft thirty years back, and we fhall find, on comparing it with the then circumfcribed ftate of the practice of Phyfic in Germany, that this treatife contains many obfervations and practical reafonings, which were then new, and which have fince actually been availed of to the great advancement of medical fcience.

The *Treatife on the Dyfentery* is uncontrovertedly acknowledged to have greatly contributed to a more improved method of treatment. There is a French tranflation of it, but to our knowledge, it has never appeared, like the treatife on Experience in Phyfic, in an Englifh drefs.

Dr. Zimmermann's fame as an able phyfician was not only now firmly eftablifhed, but he became univerfally known and admired on account of thefe various and valuable productions.

He

He held the firft rank amongft the literati; and as the great Haller, by the penetration and difcriminative patronage of a Britifh Monarch, had been honoured with the medical chair at Gottingen, fo our prefent gracious Sovereign, equally zealous to reward the confpicuous merits of Haller's avowed difciple and friend, invited Dr. Zimmermann to accept of the office of his firft phyfician at Hanover, where he was accordingly eftablifhed in that quality in 1768.

His honourable appointment at Hanover was accompanied with many advantages, and he had fondly imagined that a life free from anxiety and care would have been his conftant portion. In this expectation he however experienced a fad reverfe, and the pleafing hope which an extreme fenfibility of mind had formed, faded " like the bafelefs fabric of a vifion;" for he foon after became a prey to a fevere bodily diforder, and a martyr to the greateft irritability of the nervous fyftem.

Scarce had he arranged his domeftic houfehold at Hanover when Death, infatiate archer, aimed his relentlefs dart at the bofom of his favourite child. In the following elegant and pathetic paffages of his Effay on Solitude, he feelingly deplores the lofs of this amiable young lady.

" *Leave*

" *Leave me to myself!* I exclaimed a thoufand times, when, within two years after my arrival in Germany, I loft the lovely idol of my heart, the amiable companion of my former days. Her departed fpirit ftill hovers round me: the tender recollection of her fociety, the afflicting remembrance of her fufferings, are always prefent to my mind. What purity and innocence! What mildnefs and affability! Her death was as calm and refigned, as her life was pure and virtuous! During five long months the lingering pangs of diffolution hung continually around her. One day, as fhe reclined upon her pillow, while I read to her ' The Death of Chrift' by Rammler, fhe caft her eyes over the page and filently pointed out to me the following paffage; ' My breath ' grows weak, my days are fhortened, my heart is ' full of affliction, and my foul prepares to take ' its flight.' Alas! when I recall all thofe circumftances to my mind, and recollect how impoffible it was for me to abandon the world at that moment of anguifh and diftrefs, when I carried the feeds of death within my bofom, when I had neither fortitude to bear my afflictions nor courage to refift them, while I was yet purfued by malice and outraged by calumny, I can eafily conceive, in fuch a fituation, that my exclamation might be *Leave me to myself.*" (Page 68.) And further on, (page 85,) fpeaking of his daughter:

" Solitude

" Solitude was her world; for fhe knew no other pleafures than thofe which a retired and virtuous life affords. Submitting with pious refignation to the difpenfations of Heaven, her weak frame fuftained with undiminifhed fortitude every affliction of mortality. Mild, good, and tender, fhe endured her fufferings without a murmur or a figh: and though naturally timid and referved, fhe difclofed the feelings of her foul with all the warmth of filial enthufiafm. Diffident of her own powers fhe liftened to the precepts of a fond parent, and relied with perfect confidence upon the goodnefs of God. A malady of almoft a fingular kind, a hæmorrhage of the lungs, fuddenly deprived me of the comfort of this beloved child, even while I fupported her in my arms. Acquainted with her conftitution, I immediately faw the blow was mortal. How frequently, during that fatal day, did my wounded bleeding heart bend me on my knees before my God to implore her recovery! But I concealed my feelings from her obfervation. Although fenfible of her danger, fhe never communicated the leaft apprehenfion. Smiles arofe upon her cheeks whenever I entered or quitted the chamber. Although worn down by this fatal diftemper, a prey to the moft corroding griefs, the fharpeft and moft intolerable pains, fhe made no complaint. She mildly anfwered all my queftions

by

by fome fhort fentence, but without entering into any detail. Her decay and approaching diffolution became obvious to the eye; but to the laft moment of her life, her countenance preferved a ferenity correfpondent to the purity of her mind and the affectionate tendernefs of her heart. She had been the fubmiffive victim of ill health from her earlieft infancy; her appetite was almoft gone when we left Switzerland, a refidence which fhe quitted with her ufual fweetnefs of temper, and without difcovering the fmalleft regret, although a young man, as handfome in his perfon as he was amiable in the qualities of his mind, the object of her firft, of her only affection, a few weeks afterwards put an end to his exiftence in defpair.

" The few happy days we paffed at Hanover, where fhe was much refpected and beloved, fhe amufed herfelf by compofing religious prayers, which were afterwards found among her papers, and in which fhe implores Death to afford her a fpeedy relief from her pains: during the fame period fhe wrote alfo many letters, always affecting, and frequently fublime. They were filled with expreffions of the fame defire fpeedily to re-unite her foul with the author of her days. The laft words my dear, my well-beloved child uttered, amidft the moft painful agonies, were thefe: " To-day I fhall tafte the joys of Heaven!"

The

The fedentary life Dr. Zimmermann led, and the mental anguifh he laboured under, brought on the moft alarming fymptoms of a fevere and painful diforder, firft contracted at Gottingen. To procure relief from this inveterate malady he fubmitted to a chirurgical operation, which was performed upon him at Berlin in 1771, and which afforded fome refpite from its acrimony; and he appears afterwards to have paffed his time tolerably well at Hanover. Here it was he enjoyed the reward due to his tranfcendent abilities; hence his fame fpread over the whole literary world; here his fuperior talents were called into action and exerted; and his acquaintance courted by all whofe good fortune it was to be known to him. With many of the moft intelligent men of his time he kept up an extenfive and interefting correfpondence, chiefly on medical and philofophical fubjects; among thefe were Dr. Tiffot, Profeffor Bonnet, Dr. Marcard, Dr. Lettfom, and the learned and celebrated Mr. de Luc, at this time refident at Windfor and reader to her majefty.

To add to his celebrity, and to raife him ftill more in the circle of fociety, the truly illuftrious Northern Princefs, already mentioned, the enlightened Catherine, conferred on him another mark of her favour, by invefting him with the title of Knight of the order of St. Wolodimir

in

in 1786. This auguſt Empreſs correſponded frequently and familiarly with Dr. Zimmermann, and he has given us in his writings copies of ſome of her letters, which well deſerve to be peruſed by thoſe who, too apt to be led away by popular prejudice, are inclined to think harſhly of that moſt eminent princeſs, whoſe acts of munificence outſhine the richeſt jewel in her imperial diadem.

Recollecting on this occaſion the before adduced diſtinguiſhing proof of the Empreſs's approbation of his Eſſay on Solitude, we have ſtill, reſpecting that work, to inform our readers, that it was not till about this time (1785) that Dr. Zimmermann publiſhed the laſt or fourth volume.—The edition of 1773 comprehended only the two firſt, and a ſubſequent publication, the third. The appearance in detached parts of this ſublime performance gave riſe to ſeveral unmerited and partial repreſentations of it, and two particular publications on Solitude appeared, one in 1775, and the other in 1781, by J. H. Obereit, ſtrongly reprobating Zimmermann's Eſſay, which this ſuperficial critic conſidered as a ſcandalous and unphiloſophical attack upon, and condemnation not only of the holy retirements of the cloiſter, but likewiſe of all ſolitude in general. The Engliſh reader, on comparing this account with the Eſſay on Solitude he is acquainted with,

b will

will be apt to queſtion the intellects of Mr. Obereit, but he will recollect that this premature judgment was chiefly founded on Zimmermann's reſearches into the abuſes and miſchiefs which have ariſen in the world from the ſolitary lives of fanatics, and on which he expatiates through great part of the two firſt volumes, while the latter part of the work only, which treats of the pleaſures and advantages derived from retirement, forms the principal cón- tents of our Engliſh verſion ; the other part having, as before remarked, been ſuppreſſed in the French tranſlation, from which this was taken. In the liſt of Dr. Zimmermann's works (page vi.) our readers will have obſerved *Meditations on Solitude*, 8vo. Zurick, 1756. This ſmall work, which was con- tained in 181 pages, is engrafted in the larger one on that ſubject, and does not therefore require a particular account. Dr. Zimmermann, in the 8th chapter of the latter, which is the firſt of the 3d volume of the German original, mentions thoſe Meditations as the foundation of the more extenſive work he was then engaged in : " With a weak and juvenile pen," he ſays, with ſingular diffidence, " I recommended in that performance a proper and ſenſible enjoyment of the fleeting moments of life, and the moſt likely means to make a profitable employ of the moſt important ſciences ; I interwove in it the enthuſiaſtic love of religion and virtue, which I have always endeavoured to make the guide

of

of my steps. I wrote this fmall book in the moft beautiful feafon of the year, in a remote and filent part of my paternal dwelling, where no founds affailed my ear, where no objects diverted my attention, except the tender cooing of a folitary pair of doves."

Our author enjoyed in an eminent degree the efteem and confidence of Frederic the late King of Pruffia. On the fixth of June 1786, that great monarch and diftinguifhed hero, declining under the accumulated weight of age, the gradual decay of his bodily powers, and a dropfical complaint of long ftanding, addreffed a letter to Dr. Zimmermann, requefting to know, whether he could make it convenient to come to Potfdam to attend him as phyfician. His Majefty received an anfwer in the affirmative, in confequence of which the Doctor was further honoured with a preffing invitation, and he accordingly took his departure, and arrived at Potfdam late in the evening of the 23d of June, and early on the following morning was fent for to the King. Frederic's cafe was decidedly a dropfy, although he could not be brought to believe it, and Dr. Zimmermann was convinced from the firft day of his attendance that his Majefty was irrecoverable; efpecially on account of his intractability as a patient, and his

great.

great indulgence in melons and other things the moſt prejudicial. He waited conſtantly on his royal patient every morning, and in theſe interviews held many converſations of the moſt intereſting nature with that great and valiant potentate. For his ſervices and the expences of his journey he received two thouſand crowns, and took his leave of Potſdam on the 11th of July, deeply affected with the laſt words of the king, addreſſed to him, and which were, " Adieu, my good, my dear Dr. Zimmermann ; do not forget the old man whom you have ſeen here." Thirty-eight days after his departure, Frederic II. juſtly called the *Great*, breathed his laſt, and left the world a brilliant example of heroiſm and wiſdom, of philoſophy and philanthropy, indelibly recorded, not only in the annals of time, but in the grateful and patriotic hearts of the poſterity of his fellow ſoldiers ,and fellow countrymen, his ſubjects.

In a little time after this mournful event, Dr. Zimmermann publiſhed an *Account of his Converſations* on the above-mentioned occaſion *with the King of Pruſſia*. This account is peculiarly intereſting and entertaining, as it comprehends almoſt every ſubject which the enlightened mind of the Pruſſian monarch and of his celebrated phyſician thought worthy of conſideration.

tion. A good Englifh verfion of this book appeared very foon after.

In 1788 our elegant and fenfible writer publifhed a *Treatife on Frederic the Great,* which paffed through four editions in the fhorteft fpace of time. This work was written with a view to defend the memory of that illuftrious character, and to clear it from the afperfions which were wantonly thrown out by Count Mirabeau in his book *on the Pruffian Monarchy.* Soon after that writer publifhed his *Secret Hiftory of the Court of Berlin,* which was even more illiberal than the former; Dr. Zimmermann, therefore, enlarged his preceding work into an ample vindication of that much wronged prince from the unmerited infinuations of his calumniator, and produced it under the title of *Select Views of the Life, Character, and Reign of Frederic the Great, King of Pruffia.* This production was tranflated into Englifh in 1792 in a fuperior ftyle by Major Newman of the Naffau Guards.

It is now the painful province of the biographer to record, that from this period Dr. Zimmermann's health yielded under the ftruggle between his feelings and his duty; in the faithful difcharge of which, his attention had been always unremitting. Numberlefs muft have been the heart-

rending

rending fcenes that prefented themfelves, to the
laft degree agonizing to a man fo truly compaffionate and fympathetic as was this great philan-
thropift: and it is therefore no wonder that his
health at length gave way under their combined
operation. . Add to this, his continued and favourite occupation of writing, which was his only
recreation for the laft ten or fifteen years of his
life. Thefe gradually undermined a conftitution
of a texture naturally flight, and the difeafe, by
which it was fo materially weakened, gained upon
him daily, and at laft even fo as to affect the faculties
of his mind; which, however great and comprehenfive, from being continually upon the ftretch,
funk under the afflictive burden, and relaxed
into that melancholy ftate of intellectual debility,
which has but too frequently proved the lot of
enlarged minds after an uncommon and un-
bounded career of fcientific glory.

The fame caufes to which we attribute a bright
funfhine of genius have often been found event-
ually to produce thofe clouds which have overwhelmed the evening of a glorious day. An
exquifite delicacy of the ftructure of the organs
of fenfe and feeling is fuch, that although it
beftows a higher degree of penetration and
judgment, it ftill makes them the fooner relax
by over-exertion, while thofe of a groffer texture,
and

and of a formation lefs refined, conftantly retain
their ordinary powers entire and unimpaired.

The hypochondriac turn to which men of
great learning and fenfibility are peculiarly liable,
manifefted itfelf in the fubject of thefe memoirs
even while at Gottingen: and fuch is its fatal
power, that when once it obtains the fmalleft
hold on the human mind, there is nothing can
reftore it to its former tenfion. It is increafed
by every intervening finifter accident, however
trifling; and hence Zimmermann, who doubtlefs
experienced many fevere domeftic and perfonal
misfortunes, felt far more than the generality of
mankind under fimilar circumftances. The fuperiority of his underftanding and the greatnefs
of his genius were here of no avail : leffer minds
would have medicined private grief by the confideration of public honours. But Zimmermann
was not thus to be compenfated for a body labouring under the pangs of difeafe, and a mind
fmarting under the agonizing ftrokes of domeftic
affliction. The diftinguifhed honours conferred
upon him by three of the greateft potentates
of the earth; the various other well-earned fruits
of his extraordinary celebrity, afforded him no
fatisfaction; anxiety and difeafe tortured him by
turns, and overwhelmed every profpect ! With

b 4   him,

him, all was dark! With him, " How widowed
every thought of every joy!"

The fits of melancholy and anxiety which invariably
accompany the difpofition of mind and frame of
body already defcribed, and with which Dr. Zimmermann was affailed from time to time, began
early in 1795 to affume a very unfavourable appearance. The defpondency which had long oppreffed him was increafed, by the diftreffing circumftance of his much beloved wife being feized
with a violent fit of illnefs. His anxiety became
exceffive, and prevented him from liftening to the
confoling prognoftications of the favourable ter-
mination of her, diforder. He had fo often feen
the moft fanguine expectations defeated ; he had
fo often been the victim of delufive hope, that
his mind, already deprived of the greateft part of
its energy, refufed to admit any confoling ideas.

About this time the political hemifphere, to the
ftudy of which he had devoted a confiderable degree of attention during the latter period of his
literary life, became more and more embroiled and
obfcure.

The deftructive deluge of barbarifm and anarchy
that now recoiled from the conquered provinces of
the Roman Empire back to the inhofpitable regions,

gions, whence in the fourth century it had emana-
ted, threatened to overwhelm the whole of civilized
Europe. Fears were entertained for the safety
of Hanover; and Dr. Zimmermann, who nourish-
ed and professed the utmost detestation for these
disturbers of mankind, in the extreme perturbation
of mind into which he was now fallen, felt excef-
sively alarmed, and he could not conquer his dread
of persecution, to which his stedfast and known
adherence to the principles of religion and of integrity might possibly subject him. In his heated
imagination, the evils of an invasion of the French
were aggravated, if possible, even beyond the hor-
ror and dismay which those sons of rapine and deftruction uniformly spread around them, wherever
their baleful career conducted their sanguinary
footsteps.

" Oh what a noble mind was here o'erthrown!"

In this deplorable state, and plunged in the deepest
melancholy, it was judged advisable to try the effect
of a change of air, and an excursion to Eutin
was accordingly recommended.

Dr. Zimmermann passed two or three months in
that charming retirement in the company of his
friend Count Stolberg. It however produced no
material alteration for the better, for on his return

to Hanover in July 1795, when all fears of the enemy had subsided, his erratic ideas took another turn, and his insanity appears to have been perfectly confirmed.

Here, with Dr. Marcárd of Oldenburg, we sincerely reprobate the unavailing and disagreeable recital of the various and melancholy instances of a deranged brain, which Dr. Wichman, the physician who attended this celebrated man during his last illness, has thought fit to make public. He has given a puerile and disgusting detail of the wanderings of a ruined mind; and he has uttered them in a way as if he wished them to serve as data whence to form conclusions respecting the life and character of the sufferer. Surely an impenetrable veil ought rather to have been thrown over this scene of abased humanity! over this degradation of the human soul! Is it not enough that we behold with awful sorrow, the outlines of the dark picture, but must we be made acquainted with all the minutiæ of the distressing scene? Is it not enough for the awakening of solemn reflection, that we view the silent repositories of the dead, and the mouldering marble that announces the universal decay of every sublunary thing, but must we also rake into the loathsome and festering clay that once was man?

How affecting to reflect on this great example of the weaknefs of human nature! " Why," fays this obfervant philofopher, who lived to become a memorable inftance of the frailty he deplores; " Why fhould we pride ourfelves upon our under-ftanding, when the fineft intellects are liable to be deranged by the moft trivial phyfical accidents? Independent of external circumftances; a little extraneous air in the bowels, or an indigeftible lump in the ftomach, and lo, the divine light of the foul is extinguifhed!" (Page 253.)

His mental diforder was now accompanied with the moft excruciating agonies of body; he vifibly declined from day to day, and the virulence of his malady was greatly heightened by his utter repugnance to the taking of the medicines prefcribed. He likewife contracted an abhorrence of all food, and obftinately refufed to take a fufficient quantity of aliment for the fuftenfion of life.

This unhappy turn produced a frightful ema-ciation, fo that from a tolerably corpulent man his body became literally a mere fkeleton. To cut fhort this diftrefling narrative, he wafted away till the 7th of October 1795, when all the powers of life failing, he expired without the leaft agitation, feem-ingly, wholly worn down by the inceffant operation

3 of

of the complicated maladies of mind and of body under which he laboured.

For fome days previous to the clofe of his exiftence, it does not appear that he gave any proofs of a bewildered mind, and it fhould feem that the total debility of his natural powers had in fome degree contributed to reftrain the wanderings of his imagination. His laft words, addreffed to Dr. Wichman,' with an emphatic preffure of the hand, were, "Laiffez moi feul; je me meurs." And refigning his breath with the utmoft calmnefs, he feemed, as Seneca faid, *Potius e vita migrare quam mori.*

In the preceding pages we have already difcuffed his merits as an author. He was in every refpect an elegant and emphatic writer ; the only fault we are inclined to admit, is a kind of redundancy of expreffion, arifing from the fire and force of his language, that fometimes declined into tautology. He is likewife fuppofed to have written too much of himfelf, and to have made ufe of the firft perfon with too great a profufion in his writings ; he was himfelf fenfible of this defect, and has in many paffages either tranfiently, or more at large, hinted his inducements for "converfing familiarly," as he expreffes it, "with his readers." He wrote, as he felt, from the genuine impulfe of a benevolent

heart,

heart, which did not admit of the formal fetters of a fcholaftic precifion of ftyle. In rejecting, how-ever, the application of thefe rules, it is only for writers like Zimmerm ann, who captivate with re-fiftlefs, energy the minds and the hearts of their readers, to be allowed to fhine, greatly eccentric. Thus, nobody feels the egotifm of Cæfar's cele-brated laconic epiftle of *veni, vidi, vici,* on account of the fuperior greatnefs of the writer, of the fubject, and of the fentiment; but when Caligula fends a handful of cockle-fhells and pebbles to the Roman fenate with " behold the fpoils which *I* have achiev-ed on the ocean, behold the proofs of *my* conqueft of the iflands of Britain," who does not ridicule and defpife the egregious egotifm and effrontery of the Imperial buffoon ?

We are given to underftand that he left many unfinifhed pieces behind him, which, it is much to be regretted, he did not live to complete. Thefe are now configned to oblivion; for by his will he ordered them all to be deftroyed, and exprefsly prohibited the publication of any pofthumous works. It is, however, to be wifhed, that his extenfive and valuable correfpondence with fo many literary cha-racters of the firft rank, may, in part, be rendered public; his letters would certainly afford an abund-ant fource of pleafure to the fcientific mind; and we hope that thofe who are poffeffed of thefe pre-

cious

cious reliquiæ will not feel any repugnance to felect and publifh fuch of them as are adapted to meet the eye of the world.

As a phyfician, Zimmermann attained great ho-nour. In general it was fuppofed he followed the practice of Tiffot : but he always was the firft to adopt any new difcovery whenever he became fen-fible of its utility, and never, as many of the faculty are accufed of doing, rejected improvement as in-novation.

Upon the whole, Dr. Zimmermann much improved the practical part of the medical fcience at Hanover. During the laft ten or fifteen years of his life, we have already remarked, he chiefly confined him-felf to his defk and ftudy. Yet he conftantly de-voted two hours every morning to attendance on his patients ; befides being often abroad during the day. The leaft apprehenfion of danger called him inftantly away, and his compaffionate and fenfible heart made him difregard every thing for the fake of relieving his fellow creatures.

Whenever he beheld the convulfions of expiring nature, he moft cordially fympathized with the fuf-ferer ; and this feeling and tender difpofition was not a little prejudicial to his health. On this fub-ject we are led to quote his own words (page 32,

English

Englifh Tranflation of Solitude): " A phyfician, if he poffeffes fenfibility, muft, in his employment to ·relieve the fufferings of others, frequently forget his own. But alas! when fummoned, and obliged to attend, whatever pain of body or of mind he may endure, in maladies which are perhaps beyond the reach of his art, how much oftener muft his own fufferings be increafed by thofe which he fees others feel." And again (page 75): " At the bed of ficknefs, when I behold the efforts which the foul makes to oppofe its impending diffolution from the body, and difcover by the increafing tortures the rapid advances of approaching death; when I fee my unhappy patient extend his cold and trembling hands to thank the Almighty for the fmalleft mitigation of his pains; when I hear the utterance checked by intermingled groans; and view the tender looks, the filent anguifh of attending friends; all my powers abandon me; my heart bleeds, and I tear myfelf from the forrowful fcene, only to pour my tears more freely over the unhappy. fufferings of humanity, to lament my own inability, and the vain confidence placed in a feeble art."

It has been unjuftly inferred, from the fatirical and fevere ftyle of fome of his writings, that his temper and converfation abounded with the overflowings of vindictive fpleen. -- But here he has been

wronged

wronged indeed! He wrote only to crimfon the cheek of error, and to fhow vice its own feature; he was, on the contrary, diftinguifhed by an urbanity of manners, and an amenity and mildnefs of behaviour, the very reverfe of the farcaftic fpirit difplayed in his works, and which is levelled at the vices and follies of the world; but when they obtruded upon his notice in fociety, they were ever treated with the moft Chriftian meeknefs as frailties of human nature, deferving of compaffion and regret.

The exemplary piety and firm belief in Chriftianity, which breathe throughout his writings wherever he treats of religious fubjects, originated in a thorough conviction of the truth of the belief he profeffed, and in a free and candid enquiry into the grounds of Gofpel doctrine. His was indeed found philofophy; it did not lead him aftray into the paths of fcepticifm and of error; whither the delufive meteors arifing from fuperficial inveftigation have bewildered fo many, otherwife great and diftinguifhed minds. He obferved every moral as well as every religious duty; he was beneficent and charitable from principle, as well as from nature; and the fame law of Chrift, which inculcated the exercife of thefe duties, commanded him likewife to forbear the oftentatious difplay of them.

If

If we rightly conftrue the fcanty hints we have been able to colleƐ from his writings, Dr. Zimmermann was twice married. By his firft wife, to whom he was united in Switzerland, he had feveral children. The lady who lived to deplore his lofs was, we believe, married to him in 1782 at Hanover. For this amiable companion of his laft days, he was indebted to the friendfhip of Madame Doring, wife of the Counfellor of State of that name, and daughter of the celebrated Vice Chancellor Strube; to this lady he has dedicated his Effay on Solitude. " It was you," he fays in this Dedication, " my ever efteemed friend, that fo happily chofe for me the amiable and beloved companion of the end of my life, and whom you brought with you to Hanover, when after an abfence of eight months you returned to complete the kindeft offices of friendfhip in making me happy with the deferving woman you had always wifhed I was united to, and whom you then made me acquainted with."

His friendfhip and gratitude towards Madame Doring may be traced in the very cordial effufions of his mind, page 70 of the Englifh tranflation of Solitude; where, fpeaking of himfelf, he fays,— " Reprefent to yourfelf an unfortunate foreigner placed in a country where every one was fufpicious of his charaƐer, borne down by misfortune from every fide, attacked every moment by defpair, and,

during

during a long courfe of years, unable either to
ftoop or fit to write without feeling the moft excruciating pains ; in a country where, in the midft
of all his afflictions, he was deprived of the object
which was deareft to him in the world. Yet it
was in fuch a country, and under thefe circumftances, that he, at length, found a perfon who extended the hand of affection towards him ; whofe
voice, like a voice from heaven, faid to him, "Come,
I will dry your tears, I will heal your wounded
heart, be the kind comforter of your fufferings,
enable you to fupport them, banifh the remembrance of forrow from your mind, and recall your
fenfibility. I will endeavour to charm away the
filence of difguft by entertaining converfation, and,
when tranquillity returns, collect for you all the
flowers which adorn the paths of life ; difcourfe
with you on the charms of virtue ; think of you
with love ; treat you with efteem ; rely upon you
with confidence ; prove to you that the people
among whom you are fituated, are not fo bad as
you conceive them ; and perhaps that they are
not fo at all. I will remove from your mind all
anxiety about domeftic concerns ; do every thing
to relieve and pleafe you : you fhall tafte all the
happinefs of an eafy tranquil life. I will dili-
gently endeavour to point out your faults, and you,
in gratitude, fhall alfo correct mine : you fhall form
my mind, communicate to me your knowledge, and
preferve

preferve to me, by the affiftance of God and your own talents, the felicities of my life, together with thofe of my hufband and my children: we will love our neighbours with the fame heart, and unite our endeavours to afford confolation to the afflicted, and fuccour to the diftreffed."

Zimmermann's perfonal appearance was impreffive and noble; he was above, what is termed, the middle fize, and rather inclining to corpulence; his countenance was manly and open, with an expref-five and keen eye which beamed intelligence. He poffeffed a perfuafive and modulated voice, and in his language, whether German or French, both of which he fpoke with equal fluency, he united both energy and force with harmony and polifhed expreffion.

Such was the man we have attempted to def-cribe; as fuch our readers will venerate his me-mory, and drop over his afhes a tear of gra-titude and concern !

It is in the mean time, until an hiftorian furnifhed with more correct and more copious information fhall favour the public with a complete biography of this celebrated character, that thefe few memoirs, collected in a country, which, notwithftanding Dr. Zimmermann's connections with it, is to him a fo-reign

reign one, and in a very circumfcribed fpace of time, are offered to the world as an introduction to this work, the intrinfic merit whereof, in its original language, has procured the greateft eulogiums from the beft judges; whence it is hoped the tranflation will be perufed with fome degree of pleafure, and if it may be allowed to form a companion to the Effay on Solitude, it will be confidered as the moft flattering mark of approbation which an indulgent Public can poffibly beftow upon it.

CONTENTS.

d   XIV. Of

NATIONAL PRIDE.

CHAPTER THE FIRST.

OF NATIONAL PRIDE IN GENERAL.

T HERE is no paſſion more univerſal than Pride, It pervades all orders of ſociety : from the throne to the cottage, every individual in ſome point or other conceives himſelf ſuperior to the reſt of his ſpecies, and looks down with contempt or haughty compaſſion on all who are placed beneath his ima-ginary ſuperiority. Every nation contemplates itſelf through the medium of ſelf-conceit, and draws concluſions to its own advantage, which individuals adopt to themſelves with complacency, becauſe they confound and interweave their private with their national character. The inhabitants of moſt countries, great or ſmall, powerful or otherwiſe, value, themſelves upon a certain ſomething, of which they believe themſelves to be excluſively poſſeſſed, and are apt to view every thing that re-lates to this particular point of honour, both in themſelves and others, with prejudice and prepoſſeſ-

B   ſion.

fion. Thus humility, which forbids afcribing to ourfelves greater worth than we really poffefs, and
equity, which enjoins us to beftow the tribute of
praife wherever it is due, have with refpect to
the judgment paffed by nations upon each other
become antiquated virtues. A powerful ftate may
overawe, may deftroy the independence of its
weaker neighbour, but can never bring its inhabitants to be humble; every thing elfe may be taken
away, but their good opinion of themfelves will
remain. The Doge of Genoa, who had the honour of fubmiffively begging pardon of the haughty
Lewis the fourteenth in his palace at Verfailles, for
the trouble that Prince had been put to in bom-
barding his native city, faw nothing, amidft all the
fplendor of that magnificent court, fo worthy of
admiration, as the Doge himfelf.

National advantages are either imaginary or
real: in the former cafe, when a nation unjuftly
pretends to the poffeffion of great advantages, its
pride is arrogance; in the latter, the pride arifing
from the confcioufnefs of poffeffing greater worth
than others, when well founded, may be called a
noble pride, which arrogance can never be; for
that always implies an unjuft, an overweening, preference of ourfelves. [Self-efteem proceeds from a
fenfe of our own imaginary or real perfections, contempt for others from a fenfe of their imaginary or

real

real defects; and the union of thefe two fentiments in the mind, by the partial comparifon which a nation makes between the advantages it poffeffes, or believes itfelf to poffefs, and the deficiencies of other countries in the fame refpects, begets national pride.]

The nature of my fubject requires uncommon liberality of fentiment, and the strictest regard to equity, to avoid giving any reafonable caufe of complaint againft me. It is an arduous and difficult undertaking to attack men in their tendereft point, to delineate with forcible ftrokes the foibles and ridiculous characteriftics of the moft confiderable nations, and, penetrating through the exterior appearances and prejudices of mankind, to lay before the reader a true picture of their actions and motives, fo as not to offend any one, and to fteer at an equal diftance between the oppofite extremes of fawning flattery and wanton fatire.

Mifinterpretations, I am aware, can hardly be avoided. I may often appear to exemplify a national foible by that which may have been remarkable in one of its individuals; yet to allege, on that account, that I draw general inferences from few and partial obfervations, or that I caft on a whole nation the odium refulting from the defects of a few perfons, would be doing me injuftice. I believe I have not

offended

offended any man of underftanding; and the fenfible part of mankind in every country, I am fure,
will not take umbrage at the expofure of the weak-
neffes which tarnifh the better qualities of its inhabitants.

Illuftrious charaƈters of all profeffions are every
where to be met with; and, in this work, I defend the juft claims of all nations to common fenfe
and a good underftanding, againft the felfifh monopoly which has been exercifed by the vanity of
a few. I efteem and love perfons of merit of whatever clime or religion, and glory in their regard;
but this does not prevent my cenfuring as ridiculous whatever really is fo among the generality of
their countrymen: this remark may peculiarly be
applied to what I fay refpeƈting the Spaniards. It
would be to form from my writings a very improper idea of my real fentiments, and of the whole
tenour of my life, to fuppofe that I entertain an averfion to the Engiifh, whom I hold to be the wor-
thieft nation of the globe, notwithftanding the ill
I have to fay of them: amidft all my cenfures, I
love the French, and highly refpeƈt many individuals among them: the Italians too are well worthy
of my regard, on account of the fertility of their genius and the vivacity of their conceptions: yet
none of thefe nations will I fpare.

A re-

A remark in a certain Paris review, though it made me fmile, requires fome explanation to the public. It ftates, that I have not indifcriminately paffed my fatirical cenfure on all nations; that I ought to have looked nearer round me, and might full as eafily have traced in Germany, inftances of the fame ridiculous pride with which I made myfelf fo merry when I find it in the French, the Spaniard, or the Englifh, if I had but deigned to caft an eye on the circle more immediately within my own obfervation.

Inftances of the moft laughable perfonal pride, it is true, are plentifully to be met with in the German univerfities, in the German cities, in the German nobility, and in fhort in every thing that may be called German; but inftances of filly national pride occur but very feldom in people, who defpife the works of their own artifts, who give the preference to foreign manufactures and to foreign learning, and occafionally confole themfelves by a comparifon with the petty nation of the Swifs. With what affurance could I have expofed the flight traces of national pride to be met with among the honeft Germans, when one of the moft learned men of our age reproaches them with the want of this ufeful folly as a very great national defect? This gentleman fays, in his preface to the hiftory of the frogs, " In Europe there exifts a great nation, diftinguifhed by laborioufnefs and induftry, poffeffing men of inven-

B 3   tive

tive faculties and of great genius in as great a number as any other, little addicted to luxury, and the
moſt valiant among the brave. This nation neverthelefs hates and defpifes itfelf, purchafes, praifes,
and imitates only what is foreign ; it imagines that no
drefs can be elegant, no food or wine delicious or
even palatable, no dwelling commodious, unlefs
ſtuff, taylor, clothes, cook, wine, furniture, and
architect, come to it at an exceſſive expence from
abroad ; and what adds a zeſt to all, from a country inhabited by its natural enemies. This fingular
nation exalts and praifes foleIy and above meafure
the genius and wit of foreigners, the poetry of foreigners, the paintings of foreigners ; and efpecially with regard to literature, foreign books written
in the moſt miferable ſtyle are folely purchafed,
read, and admired by thefe infatuated people, who
know little even of their own hiſtory, fave from the
faulty, unfaithful, and malicious relations of foreign authors."

Let others decide on the juſtice of this well-
meant reproach ; for me it only remains to inform
the Parifian cenfor, that I am really no German,
although I write German, and yield, in his opinion,
to none in the humility with which I addrefs the
Auſtrian and Swabian nobility, according to the
cuſtom of the country, ufing the title of Gracious
Lord, and feem to him to facrifice truth at the
ſhrine of fervile adulation.

CHAPTER THE SECOND.

OF INDIVIDUAL PRIDE, AND THE PRIDE OF DIFFERENT CLASSES.

Folly is the queen of the world, and we all, more or lefs, wear her livery, her ribands, her ftars, and her bells. Moft men, being partial to themfelves, efteem only their own image in others. The predominancy of vanity among mankind is what caufes the number of the proud to be fo great, fince it is from vanity that all pride arifes, while felf-conceit which begets this vanity is by no means originally implanted in human nature, like that neceffary felf-love, which incites every creature to attend to its own prefervation. It feems rather an adventitious quality which muft have arifen in a ftate of fociety, when the mind became capable of comparing itfelf with others, and which, in confequence, has been interwoven with our other affumed opinions, and pervades all our actions and motives. We generally have too good an opinion of our perfonal qualities, not to take pleafure in comparing ourfelves with others; and the man of fenfe equally with the fool entertains the fame complacent ideas of himfelf, founded on this comparifon; only in the laft it is

B 4   always

always more abfurd, in proportion to the futility
and injuftice of his parallel.

Self-conceit begets arrogance, haughtinefs,
vanity, frivolity, and oftentation, and appears in
various fhapes, according to the difference it meets
with in the natural intellects, in the mode of education and of living, in the fociety, in the ftation,
and in the rank, and fortune, of men. In little
minds, whatever form it affumes, it is always folly;
in minds more enlightened, it fometimes is linked
with knowledge; in all, it fubfifts either openly or
in fecret at the expence of others, efpecially where
it is the only antidote againft the malice with
which a number of fools depreciate one wife man.

The felf-conceit of every one muft of neceffity
clafh with that of his neighbour, and of courfe increafe by oppofition; for whoever is not as much
valued by others, as he thinks he deferves, efteems
himfelf the more, by comparing their fuppofed ignorance with his ideal worth; while, by openly con-
temning his competitor, this laft is likewife induced
to fall into the fame train of thinking with refpect
to his own advantages, which he, by the fame
mode of arguing, conceives to be fuperior to thofe
of his neighbour, for exactly the fame reafon.
Self-conceit too opens the way to an irrefiftible
fatisfaction, by the tacit agreement which mankind

feem to have entered into, that each fhall love in a certain degree in another what they think worthy of admiration in themfelves. Now, as in both cafes felf-conceit in a lively temper becomes a paffion, it leads us into innumerable errors, fince paffion always affects our fight in fuch a way, that we fee but one fide of the picture, in which too we are fure to behold no more than we chufe.

We always return to the confideration of our dear felves, juft as the imagination of a lover is ever recurring to the contemplation of his miftrefs; he neither fees nor regards any thing but the object of his affection. So too the felf-admirer is blind and deaf to all but his own aftonifhing perfections; he is provoked at whatever does not exactly coincide with his ideas of them, and fuppofes that his own conviction of their exiftence is fufficient to render them equally difcernible to all: as fome years ago, a young Englifh inamorato, poffeffed with the true fpirit of Quixotifm, conftrained our inoffenfive country people whom he met with in the fields round Laufanne, to confefs that a certain young lady of Geneva, whom he named to them, was the moft lovely of her fex, by threatening them with the point of his fword.

Loving ourfelves beyond all others, fo we think ourfelves entitled to the firft place, and believing

our

our way of thinking on all points to be perfectly right, we consequently look upon our judgment as more found, and our penetration as more
subtle, than the judgment or penetration of
such as deviate from our received opinions : with
regard to such as agree with us, we only esteem
them as representing ourselves; and, misled by these
selfish notions, we wish to be regarded in the same
pleasing light by others as we look on ourselves;
but experience, alas ! teaches us that our thoughts,
our opinions, and our sentiments, please others only
in so far as they accord with their own ; for this
reason our vanity forces us to esteem in others that
coincidence of opinion which assures us of their
esteem, while we cannot avoid hating the contra-
riety of their sentiments to ours; because we most
certainly know, that they for the same reason either
hate or at least despise us : and again, many people,
averse to disturb the repose they enjoy in the downy
lap of self-complacency, never take the trouble to
investigate the opinions of others, or to weigh their
own against them ; and so, remaining ignorant of
their respective merits, go on in the beaten path of
invariably giving the preference to themselves.

These fundamental principles, deduced from nature by the most acute philosophers, and confirmed
by the daily experience of every attentive observer
of mankind, throw a light on many ludicrous ap-

pearances

pearances which are conftantly to be feen around us, or obferved in hiftory, which appears to be no other than an account of men's infirmities and defects, all which arife from felf-conceit, either with refpect to ourfelves or others.

Man looks upon himfelf as the centre to which all created beings tend. Among the pifmires inhabiting this mighty mole-hill, there have always been fome who could not difcard the idea, that the fun only fhone for them to bafk in ; that yonder ftarry worlds were nothing more than golden ftuds placed for the fake of ornament in the firmament, and that the whole of this magnificent fyftem was created folely for the fupply of their wants, the gratification of their fenfes, and the amufement of their imaginations. Many orders of men have continually flattered themfelves with the idea that they were the chief, if not the only objects of Divine Providence, and have, in confequence, afcribed innumerable effects of the general and regular courfe of things, to an immediate interpofition of the Deity, folely regarding themfelves, according as their prejudices, their paffions, their intereft, or their vanity, might incite them to believe.

The fame folly is obfervable in individuals of all ranks, for each is in his own eye a being of the greateft importance : true, he may often yield the

5 precedence

precedence to others, but that only becaufe they are
held in higher eftimation by the reft of the world, for
he is very far from refpecting them in his heart, and
the lefs on account of this mortifying pre-eminence ;
for this very reafon it is, that the individual whom
every one places immediately below himfelf in
worth, is evidently the firft of his profeffion. After
the battle of Salamis, all the commanders were enjoined to declare before the altar of Neptune upon
oath, who had conducted himfelf beft on that day ;
every one of them claimed for himfelf the firft palm ;
but they were unanimous in allotting the fecond to
Themiftocles.

All men prize above meafure their own tafte
and favourite fcience, and efteem every one who
has not a genius for that particular branch of
knowledge, as unqualified. This is carried fo far,
that men often ridiculoufly conceive the delights of
another world will be taftelefs without the enjoyment of their moft cherifhed paffion : the fportf-
man believes that when he is freed from the narrow
bounds of this nether world, his fpirit will be eter-
nally happy in following the pleafures of the chace,
from one planet to another, through the whole ex-
panfe of heaven ; and the alchymift entertains no
doubt but that the elect will be bleffed to all eternity,
in the perufal and contemplation of Paracelfus. To
adduce but one inftance, Le Sack, a famous
French

French dancing mafter during the reign of queen Anne, in great admiration once afked a friend, whether it were true that Mr. Harley was made an Earl and Lord Treafurer; and finding it confirmed, faid, ' " Well, I wonder what the devil the queen could fee in him; for I taught him to dance two years, and he was the greateft looby that ever I had to do with."

Self-conceit always exalts a man above his proper level, and perverts his right perception of the fitnefs of things. Every prince muft have his court days and his ambaffadors be his dominions three miles or three hundred in extent; every nobleman his attendants and pages, whether his revenue juftifies fuch oftentation or not; and every fhopkeeper's wife, whether fhe fells tape by the yard or pins by the hundred for fix days, muft on the feventh, be a fine lady. A blockhead will ever extol the depth of his penetration; the knave his honefty; the blind follower of a particular religious tenet his thorough conviction of its infallibility; the hypocrite his piety; the upftart his nobility; the demirep her virtue; the old maid her chaftity; which fhe indeed often to her forrow retains for want of it's having ever been tempted; the idle and infignificant can pertly engrofs the whole of a converfation of which they make themfelves the topic, without feeling how much they deprefs men of
fenfe

fenſe on ſuch occaſions.   There is not a youthful coxcomb in the univerſe who would barter
his head for that of the moſt eminent genius;
nor a wealthy ſcoundrel that cares for any kind of
merit but the cunning that has brought him his
riches; and no virtue can counterbalance the glittering gewgaws of coronets and embroidery in the
eyes of a titled ignoramus.   Thoſe who indulge in
ſelf-conceit generally go farther, and not only love
their opinions like themſelves, but look with ſcorn
on all who entertain different ideas, and who do
not exactly give the preference to what they eſteem
worthy of it.   The idler pities the buſy fool that
is ever immerſed in the occupations of trade; the
hunter deſpiſes the fellow that cannot talk of dogs
and horſes; the gameſter thinks thoſe who care
not for cards little better than clods; the burgo-
maſter who magiſterially gives importance to trifles,
and the counſellor who ſcribbles his deciſion on the
caſes that are brought for his conſideration with
the ſame caſe as he gulps down his wine, aſk with
haughty ſelf-ſufficiency, what good the pedant does
who can employ his time no better than to write
a book? To him who has no ſenſibility of ſoul, all
the nobler, the purer emotions of the heart, ſeem
abſurd and ridiculous; the man who does not
feel the poignancy of genuine wit ſtares at the
applauſe it excites; while on the other hand low
jokes, puns, and obſcene alluſions form a fund of
enter-

entertainment to congenial vulgar minds; to giddy girls, whofe hearts pant for a fop, and whofe lot is often a fool, the manly accomplifh- ments of knowledge, fenfe, and ferioufnefs of cha- racter, are of no worth; men of a churlifh temper look on the enchanting features, the foftly alluring eyes and graceful mien of the lovely daughters of our general mother, merely as childifh playthings, unworthy the attention of the lords of the creation ; mercenary mercantile fouls, who value a woman only by the weight of gold fhe brings with her as a portion, are incapable of conceiving how any one can be fuch a dolt as to take a wife with good fenfe, delicate feelings, and a benevolent heart, in prefe- rence to ftupidity with money ; and the captivating allurements which nature teaches a blooming girl to throw out for the grand purpofe of her creation, are inveighed againft and reprimanded as downright immodefty, by the antiquated prude, who has loft all powers of attraction.

One of the objects in which felf-conceit moft predominantly appears, is in matters of religion, and the opinion we entertain of our punctual difcharge of the religious duties incumbent on us : it is fure, in this refpect, to declare itfelf in an inexprefible contempt and pity of thofe who do not make fuch a public difplay of their piety as we do. Hardly a day paffes without the facrifice of fome innocent victim

at

at the altar of the malignant paſſions of people of
this caſt, to whom evil ſpeaking is food, cavilling
their entertainment, ſlander their delight, falſe aſ-
perſion the enlivening fire of their diſcourſe, and
malice the ſoul of their actions. Such gloomy zeal-
ots too often become the ſlaves of every vice, and
are by turns, laſcivious, gluttonous, quarrelſome,
ambitious, avaricious, hard-hearted, and cruel;
the tumults of their ſordid minds, at the loſs of a
trifle, might be compared to the uproar of chaos;
and under the cloak of devotion they ſin againſt
common honeſty : but although none are ſo punctual in attending divine ſervice, though none make
ſuch ſolemn preparations at the approach of every
religious feſtival, though the word Chriſtianity is
ever in their mouths, though they are indefatigable
in viſiting the infirm and adminiſtering ſpiritual
conſolation to thoſe whoſe ſituation would rather
require the opened hand of charity, though none
pay greater reſpect to their own clergy, though
none ſo vehemently exclaim againſt the growth of
infidelity; yet the world is not ſo effectually deceived
by their hypocritical profeſſions, as their conſciences
are lulled by their own ſophiſtications ; for every
honeſt man abhors ſuch lip-ſervice, and every wiſe
man ſmiles at their ſanctiſied hypocriſy.

Partiality of judgment, with its concomitants,
injurious contempt and cenſure, extends itſelf
through

through all characters, stations, and professions;
people of contrary dispositions, of different ages and
tastes, reciprocally think each other stupid, ridiculous, and full of imperfections: the advantages
which they respectively enjoy are the subject of
their exultation, and those they are defective in,
they cry down and disdain. Thus fools are ever
making faces at each other, and jostling their
empty noddles; and thus arise the many squab-
bles about trifles that daily occur in the world,
and in which neither party are in the right or in
the wrong.

Shallow-brained coxcombs entertain the most
marked contempt for men of genius; the former
are continually buzzing in the ears of the latter
the barren objects of their trifling observations, and
the uninteresting occurrences of their frivolous
lives; while these cannot but behold with indifference the flimsy materials which form the furniture of their senseless pates, and, sighing at the insignificancy of their conversation, turn with disgust
from the daily round of the same remarks which
neither instruct nor entertain. A vulgar mind, and
such as is only adequate to the common occupations
of life, thinks these alone useful, noble, and praise-
worthy, and the time that is otherwise employed
totally lost; he pities the conceited blockheads who
embark in literary pursuits and scientific researches,

and

and who cannot be contented with the obvious knowledge and fuch ideas as immediately prefent themfelves, without the trouble of further purfuit than looking out at the window, or walking to and fro before the door. Wife men and fools are there-fore reciprocally tirefome and infipid to each other whenever they meet, and both repay themfelves for the tormenting uneafinefs they have felt, by mutual contempt.

Profeffions likewife are animated with the fame fpirit of difdain towards each other, according to the ideas they have refpectively formed of their utility and rank in fociety : the citizen defpifes the farmer; the feaman the foldier ; the foldier the civilian ; the civilian the ecclefiaftic, and among ecclefiaftics numberlefs are the pretences adduced to countenance their mutual contempt; while the courtier expreffes his derifion of them all.

Among the learned, mutual fcorn is as common and apparent as among the moft illiterate. There are few of the former who do not prize their fa-vourite ftudy above all human knowledge, and are indifferent to every thing that does not regard their own hobby-horfe : the naturalift thinks very meanly of the etymological opinions and laborious inveftigations of the grammarian; the botanift is equally uncharitable with refpect to the ftudies of

the

the aftronomer ; the lawyer cannot bear to hear of the utility or learning of the phyfician ; and the man who, by any new contrivance, an electrical machine, an air balloon, or a diving bell, has acquired riches and a name, cannot comprehend how the world can trifle away time in empty prattle about politics. A country alehoufe-keeper-has more efteem for one fubftantial farmer, than for all the wits in Chriftendom ; the natural philofopher laughs aloud at the imbecillity of the ethic philofopher, who foolifhly fuppofes that the contemplation of the nature of men and of their actions, is of more confequence than the contemplation of the nature and actions of frogs ; the mathematician's ftandard of excellence is his rule and compaffes, his arithmetical tables, and decimal fractions, and thefe ftupid inventions again are the derifion of the metaphyfician. The queftion was once put in a mixed company at Paris, " what a metaphyfician was ?" a mathematician prefent an-fwered, " An ignorant blockhead." Let the chy-mifts, the naturalifts, the phyficians, the moralifts, and the experimental philofopher be afked, " what a mathematician is ?" they will anfwer, " An igno-rant blockhead." Profe writers have a great anti-pathy to each other ; fome pride themfelves upon the gigantic fize of their works, others on the felection and terfenefs of their fubjects ; the former rake toge-ther in their writings cart-loads of rubbifh from the affemblage of all that has been invented or heard of

fince the deluge; they are never tired of deep refearches, and fpin out their matter with the moft
patient induftry, ringing the changes of their abfurd
notions till the reader nods over them, not from a
principle of thought and acquiefcence, but lulled by
the inceffant repetition of the fame founds. Such
authors reverence their brethren who can write a
folio, while he who can only fill a duodecimo, muft
be a very poor genius indeed; for to confine
one-felf to fay no more on a fubject than is requi-
fite for its difcuffion, proves, in their opinion, a deplorable fterility of intellect; they call writings of
judgment, penetration, and elegance, unintelligible, trifling, frothy, fophiftical, French nonfenfe:
they diflike wit as eunuchs diflike love, and, being
genuine pedants, call all fuch as are endowed with
common fenfe in its purity and fimplicity, the un-
enlightened herd; while thefe, on the other hand,
think a fool's cap would be the moft proper ornament to fet off the gravity and overbearing conceit,
fo vifibly imprinted in their long and folemn vifages.
Poets think very meanly of profe writers, for profe
is the common vehicle of converfation; and when
their works, confecrated to immortality, expire before the next returning folftice after their birth, the
perverted tafte of the whole age is vehemently called
in queftion; but they likewife defpife each other,
and of all their creditors, thofe to whom they owe
a fpite are the fureft of punctual payment. As
                                                    their

their choler is confeffedly more irritable than that of any other people, fo they do not reft fatisfied with expreffing their contempt of what they think defpicable, but, as thofe who confort with wolves muft join in their howlings, fo they would oblige whoever has his character at heart, to fide with them, or fubmit to the application of that article in the laws of Solon, which declares all fuch as remain neuter in any dangerous commotion in the ftate, infamous, as not caring for the happinefs or mifery of their country, nay, even making a merit of their forbearance; on which account a poet often alternately employs, according to his humour, his pen in panegyrics and pafquinades on the fame man, who is, perhaps, to-day a man of genius or a Mecænas, and to-morrow a dunce or an Omar, who ordered the deftruction of the Alexandrian library, giving this memorable reafon, that whatever learning it contained that was not comprehended in the Alcoran, was prejudicial to the interefts of the true religion, and whatever was already written in that facred book need not be elfewhere preferved.

From all this it appears, that men flight each other from being the flaves of felf-conceit, which is avowedly the cafe with almoft every one; infignificant indeed is the number of thofe equitable minds, which

can,

can, with philofophical indifference, weigh their own advantages againft thofe of others, and obferve the lightnefs of their own balance.

The agreement or difagreement of ideas and fentiments, is the fure criterion by which to judge of the mutual efteem or contempt between the parties: whoever is much fought after by little minds, and can affociate with and pleafe the weak and ignorant, may well be fufpected of fimilar difqualifications, which is a confolatory reflection for the hatred which is generally entertained by the' ignorant againft the learned. Of a perfon we do not at all know, we form not an advantageous idea if we find he is the admiration of fools, for the centre of gravity itfelf is not fo attractive as dulnefs to its counterpart. Where the prince is a fool, that country is the paradife of fools; like the ephemeral infects of a fummer's day, the votaries of folly emerge from' their retreats, and betake themfelves to Court, the moment a foul congenial to their own afcends the throne: there they are in their element; the moft unmeritorious fycophants are advanced to the higheft dignities; all that is foolifh, vicious, and abfurd, becomes fafhionable, and is moft decidedly preferred, while merit and parts retire dejected from the fociety of men, who hate what is not made after their own image.

There

There is another caufe of partiality or contempt for men and manners, which unites with felf-conceit to beget vanity and pride; that is, the circumftances of local fituation ; the objects that furround us, the fociety, the country in which we live, and the government we are under, all influence more or lefs our thoughts, motives, and actions ; we form our ideas according as we are fituated in the above refpects, and adopt to them our opinions of the decency, truth, propriety, and beauty of every thing that comes within our obfervation.

He who has never travelled, who has read nothing, and who fhuns the converfation of thofe who have, limits his ideas to what he daily fees around him, imagines that beyond the little fpan he inhabits there is nothing but wild uncultivated defarts and gloomy wildernefles ; or forming his opinions of all that is beyond the circle of his own obfervation, by what is within it, he is like the Parifian mechanic fpoken of in the account of an excurfion from Paris to St. Cloud, who believed, that the hills bordering his view were uninhabited, and, from the horfe-chefnut trees in the publick walks at Paris, concluded, that all grain and pulfe grew likewife on trees.

From this dependency on the objects which furround us, proceeds a rooted habit of judging of diftant

things

things by the fcale of domeftic appearances, and by
the notions which prevail in our own little circle.
In Paris, for this reafon, notwithftanding all that
may be thought of it in other countries, it is by
no means an object of ridicule for five or fix city
fportfmen to go a hunting in a coach with jack-
boots, bag-wigs, guns, fwords, and piftols, who,
when they come to a proper place, take their ftands
behind fo many trees, in order to let fly at any
poor hare that may happen to run that way : for
this reafon, the negroes paint their devils white and
their god black : for this reafon, certain nations
painted the goddefs of love with monftrous breafts
hanging down almoft to her knees : and for this
fame reafon it was, that on endeavouring to make
an honeft Swifs comprehend the extent of kingly
wealth and magnificence, he afked with a proud
confcioufnefs of the importance of his ruftic riches,
" whether a king had a hundred head of cattle on
the hill ?" Whoever is of confequence in his hamlet
muft be a refpeftable perfon every where.   At the
congrefs of Baden in 1714, all the feveral plenipo-
tentiaries dined one day in public, and many people
affembled round the table out of curiofity.   Marfhal
Villars difcovered among them a very pretty young
woman from Zurich, and went up to her to give
her a kifs, when inftantaneoufly a thick-headed
crook-legged dapperling of a Zuricker, preffed forward through the crowd and cried out like a
                                        demoniac,

demoniac, " Hold, hold, Marſhal, let her alone, for ſhe is *my* ſiſter, and her huſband is *warden* of our company."

The ſmaller and more inſulated the place or ſociety is in which we live, the lower and more contracted are the opinions we form in conſequence; and when we are ignorant of every thing beyond our narrow ſphere of life, whereby to form a juſt eſtimate of things, we look upon our tenets as the only proper rule of judgment, being unacquainted with the exiſtence, much leſs with the probable merits, of any other. The more abridged a man is in his knowledge, the higher does he value himſelf, and the more inſolent does he behave towards others. He condemns every thought that does not flow from his own fruitful brain, and every action and faſhion, of which he has not ſet the example. He perſecutes as much as he can with impunity every man of genius, whom he ſuppoſes, on account of the ſuperiority of his talents, neceſſarily inimical to his manner of thinking and projects; he ſtyles an uniform coincidence with his ideas, good ſenſe; blindneſs towards his failings, friendſhip; and in any caſe, not to further his views, is treachery, and a crime; he fancies his reputation is firmly eſtabliſhed, when he is ſtared at and admired by a number of clowns; and like the commander of a ſhip, who rules over his little

wooden

wooden realm with defpótic fway, he is almoft convinced, that the axis of the globe muft quake before him, like the table which he' ftrikes in the vehemence of his rhetorick.

This defect is incurable in every man of note who inhabits a fmall town, when his mind is not more expanded than the place of his refidence ; for he who is the man of moft confideration in a little circle, will naturally deteft extenfive fociety, where he is fure to lofe his pre-eminence, he will particularly be hoftile to men of commanding underftandings, and will avoid their converfation, for his foul will fhrink from their fcrutiny. Men are infinitely more pleafed with the company of fuch as out of complaifance or ignorance accede to their abfurd propofitions, than of thofe who infinuate that they are erroneous.

The half animated oyfter, confined within its fhell, knows as much of the world, as a man involved in this intellectual mift does of the real fituation or value of things. Always furrounded by the fame objects, he will never alter his creed; he will ever efteem his own belief as an incontrovertible argument in every difpute ; he is in himfelf all in all, and thofe who hold other principles, are blinded by falfehood. Such men ever adhere to the axiom, that relative confequence is real confequence ;

quence; in vain you may put a standard into their hands to measure themselves by, they indignantly cast it away, they have forsooth already measured themselves, and must, to be sure, be great and consequential men throughout the world, for they are of weight and importance on their own dunghill. This excessive self-esteem makes them look at all other persons and things through the wrong end of the perspective glass; and the value of all who are not of their stamp is imperceptible to their perverted vision. On this account the most unimportant trifles swell in their hands to matters of great moment; and thence also proceeds their opinion, that no one ever was, or ever will be capable of rivalling them in the greatness or usefulness of their exploits. It is the prevalence of this infatuation that solely occasions the big swoln gravity, which is the soul of administration in the petty jurisdiction of all countries. Every thing must bow down and vanish before the tremendous authority of a judge of this description; when he smooths his countenance into all-sufficiency, and with an elevation of shoulders, throws his straddling legs full length before him, clears his lungs with a loud and awful hem, then graciously declines his face from the contemplation of the ceiling, and slowly bending his eyes downward, casts them with ineffable disdain on the circle of bob-wigs and uncombed locks around him, all which seem unanimously to exclaim, " the world

fure

fure muſt confeſs this man is great, for he is the
greateſt in our town-hall !"

Theſe true and unexaggerated obfervations prove,
that the generality of mankind are proud; that
felf-conceit is the fountain-head of pride; and that
pride generates the moſt ridiculous arrogance; when
ſtupidity and confined knowledge of things become
by outward circumſtances the companions of felf-
conceit.

CHAPTER THE THIRD.

OF THE PRIDE OF WHOLE NATIONS.

Wʜᴏʟᴇ nations think juſt as the generality of individuals do of their own advantages. We might ſafely conclude from the thoughts and opinions of ſingle perſons, what their combined effects are in the community they belong to, did we not alſo directly know, that every nation muſt have the ſame manner of faſhioning its ideas with the individuals who compoſe it. All hiſtories are memorials of the partiality of nations for themſelves ; the moſt civilized and the moſt ſavage people ſhew, that they believe they poſſeſs certain advantages, which they diſallow to others ; either the religious tenets they hold, their cuſtoms, their government, or ſome other peculiarity, is a pleaſing ſubject of contemplation to them. As individuals, ſo villages, cities, provinces, nations, are infected with this darling ſelf-conceit, and their own particular vain glory ; and every member of the community, by a very natural chain of ideas, takes part in the general vanity, and joins with his village or his nation in railing at other villages and nations of the world. About fifty years ago, the inhabitants of a certain ſmall vil-

lage

lage in Rheinthal, a fmall diftrict, and one of thofe
called the dependances of Switzerland, being poffeffed by all the Swifs Cantons, urged a complaint
to the judge, that the parfon had on the preceding
Sunday audacioufly uttered thefe reprehenfible
words, " that hardly one hundred fouls out of the
whole of their illuftrious community would be
faved."

Every nation is exceedingly pleafed with itfelf,
and confiders all other focieties of men, more or
lefs, as beings of an inferior nature. A foreigner
and a barbarian were fynonymous terms among
the Greeks; and were employed as fuch among the
Romans; and are ftill fo with the majority of the
French nation. It happened at the court of Zell,
in the time of the late duke, that the duchefs (who
was of the French family of d'Oibreufe) with fome
French noblemen were the only company at his
highnefs's table; one of the Frenchmen fuddenly
exclaimed, " It is very droll indeed!" " What is
fo droll?" faid the duke. " That your highnefs is
the only *foreigner* at table," was the anfwer. Even
the Greenlanders pronounce the word *Stranger*
with an air of contempt, and in fome of the towns
of the Swifs Cantons, the word *Aufburger* or alien
has the fame degrading fignification, as is exempli-
fied by the anfwer given a few years ago, by an
honeft fruiterer in one of thofe towns, to the in-
timation

timation that he received, that his daughter, a very pretty maiden, had captivated the heart of a certain German prince, " No, no," fays he, " no, no, I know better than to let my daughter have to do with an *Aufburger*."

National contempt oftener arifes from what ftrikes the fenfes than the underftanding. At Vienna, at Paris, and at Rome, a Swifs and a brute were long efteemed equivalent denominations, and to fpeak honeftly, I have myfelf felt abafhed, when at Verfailles I have compared the ftill and formal gait of the Swifs halberdiers, with the airy flippancy of the monkeys, who danced attendance at the levee. Moft people ridicule foreign manners, becaufe they differ from their own; and in this point, few are lefs blind and arrogant than the French courtiers, who, inftead of feeing in Peter the Great, a monarch of genius, who travelled for the fake of improvement, and who had defcended from his throne to attain the qualifications neceffary to enable him to fill it again worthily, beheld in him no more than a foreigner, a brute, who being ignorant of French cuftoms, and a ftranger to their affectation and grimace, ought as foon as he came among them, to have ftudied their manners, and have taken a pattern of their undiftinguifhed urbanity wherewith to civilize his Ruffian bears.

The

The mutual contempt between nations too often appears even in members of fociety who ought to be far above fuch illiberal prejudices. There are few authors who hear with temper a comparifon between the writers of their own nation and foreign literati; and let them be ever fo unfair and virulent towards each other, they are at all times ready to unite in attacking a foreigner, who fhould dare to find fault with any one among them.

The arrogant Greeks owed all their advantages, nay, their civilization, to foreigners: the Phenicians taught them the ufe of letters, inftructed them in the arts and fciences, gave them laws; the Egyptians lent them the mythology on which they built their religion; yet Greece, favoured Greece, was in their eyes, the mother of all nations. It is remarked, that the Greek hiftorians feldom make ufe of foreign names, fometimes totally omitting them, but more commonly altering them with the moft fcrupulous attention to give them a Grecian turn and a more harmonious found; and it is therefore not furprifing, that in fucceeding times, this vainglorious people adopted the perfuafion, that nearly all the other nations of the earth were colonies from Greece.

The modern Italians confidently place themfelves upon a level with the ancient Romans, without re-

flecting

ing that the defcendants of thefe conquerors of the world are the moft infignificant among the flaves of caprice and fuperftition ; or that the cities, whofe priftine fame they glory in, and even many of thofe whofe names have been renowned in the middle and latter ages, are now nearly uninhabited, and their unfrequented ftreets overgrown with weeds. Many fmall towns in the Campania of Rome were the native places of Roman confuls, generals, and emperors, and the prefent fqualid inhabitants of fuch places fpeak of them as their townfmen and relations. The peafant, who can point out the fpot where fuch or fuch an eminent character was born, firmly believes, in common with all the inhabitants round the facred barn or hog-ftye, or whatever elfe the Roman villa has been metamorphofed into, that their countryman, their progenitor, was the greateft man hiftory ever made mention of. A fingle fenator of Rome, deciding without appeal on the petty fquabbles and difputes of the loweft order of citizens, is the actual reprefentative of that tribunal to which the impreffive majefty of the ancient fenate and of the Roman people is dwindled. He has four affeffors called confervators, who are changed every quarter. Thefe confervators, as well as the fenator himfelf, are nominated by the pope, who does not even leave the Romans that remnant of liberty which many cities enjoy, even under abfolute monarchies, the free election of their own ma-

giftrates ;

giftrates; yet, neverthelefs, both the fenator and thefe confervators idly conceive themfelves the fucceflors of that auguft body whofe feats they at prefent occupy, and that they are entitled to all the refpect due to a Roman fenate, and to all its invaluable privileges, while the vicegerent of heaven himfelf muft be highly honoured by feeing at his feet that affembly before whom fo many kings and princes had bowed their necks. The Traftaverini, that is the wretched militia of the ward of Traftavera in modern Rome, the ancient *Regio Tranftiburina*, abfolutely call themfelves defcendants of the Trojans of remote antiquity, and look upon the inhabitants of the other quarters of Rome as a mob of fpurious Latians; and yet they value both, in the midft of their poverty and bigotry, as being citizens of ancient Rome, from whofe former courage and inflexibility they are fo far degenerated, that the very rare occurrence among them of the execution of a malefactor almoft frightens them into fits. All the modern inhabitants of Rome of the lower clafs, confole themfelves with the remembrance of the noble actions of their imaginary progenitors, and this makes even mifery in Rome affume the air of pride and difdain. In a tumult that had arifen there, in confequence of the high price of corn, it once happened that the fon of a poor baker's widow of the Traftavera ward was killed; the pope, who feared the worft confe-

quences

quences from the popular effervefcence encreafed
by this accident, immediately deputed a cardinal
and feveral of the nobility to fee the widow, and offer
whatever fhe required as an atonement for the injury fhe had fuftained ; to which the Roman matron indignantly replied, " I do not fell my blood."
Towards the approach of a public feftival, a whole
family fometimes pinch themfelves in every neceffary, in order to have wherewithal to ride about in a
coach. Such families as cannot, even with the utmoft
œconomy, attain the pleafure of hiring one, adopt
another expedient to exhibit themfelves : the mother dreffes herfelf in the habit of a chambermaid,
and in that charafter accompanies her daughter,
tricked out in her holiday clothes, while the father
follows in proceffion with the proper accoutrements
of a lackey.

Englifhmen themfelves acknowledge, that they
inherit from their anceftors a ftupid prepoffeffion
againft all other inhabitants of the globe. Whenever one of them is engaged in any quarrel with
a foreigner, he is fure to begin his addrefs with
fome reproachful nick-name, which he appropriates to the native country of the perfon he is con-
tending with. Foreigners are on fuch an occafion
refpeftively faluted with the appellation of *French
puppy, Italian monkey, Dutch ox,* or *German hog.*
As to the word French, the national antipa-

thy againſt their oppoſite neighbours is ſo great, that to call a foreigner, *dog*, is not inſulting enough, but he muſt be called *French dog*, to convey the higheſt degree of deteſtation. The national preju-dices of the Engliſh are alſo too conſpicuous in their conduct towards the natives of their two ſiſter king-doms, that compoſe the Britiſh empire, who live un-der the ſame king and the ſame government, and fight with them for one common cauſe. Nothing is more frequently heard in England, than, " thou beggarly Scott ;" " thou blood-thirſty impudent Iriſh lout :" and, in general, an Engliſhman well-ſtuffed with beef, pudding, and porter, heartily de-ſpiſes every other nation of Europe. The Yorkſhire fox-hunter eſteems himſelf co-equal with all the princes of the earth ; for his fox-hounds are the beſt in the whole county. An Engliſhman to be ſure, too, muſt ſolely, by being born a Briton, have an innate taſte for works of genius, and be a thorough connoiſſeur in the fine arts ; and although the pope has expreſsly prohibited the ſale of any of the paint-ings or ſculptures of famous artiſts to ſtrangers, yet theſe proud iſlanders on their viſits to Italy expend yearly as much at Rome in ſtatues and paintings as they uſed to do before ; that is to ſay, they pur-chaſe as much dawbed canvaſs and broken marble, as the money they have ſet apart for the acquiſition of curioſities will command.

Let

Let me likewife give the reader the ftatement of the parallel drawn by Englifhmen of approved learning and talents, between them and other nations, in their own ftile. They fay, " The French are polite, witty, and eafily elated, but they are a parcel of hungry flaves, and cannot call either their time, their purfes, or their perfons their own, for all is the property of their king. The Italians are without liberty, morals, or religion. The Spaniards are brave, devout, and jealous of their honour, but poor and opprefled ; and for all their bragging, that the fun never rifes or fets in the Spanifh dominions, they never dare make their freedom, learning, arts, manufactures, commerce, or achievements, the fubjects of their boafts. The Portuguefe, too, are all ignorant and fuperftitious flaves. The Germans are always either in actual war, or recovering from its devaftations. The Dutch lag behind in every virtue, are deeply funk in avarice, and are only roufed from their natural fupinenefs, to take an active part in trade, by the luft of gain. Switzerland is fcarcely perceptible in the map of the world ; and to draw our attention, the virtues of the Swifs ought to fhine forth with the luftre of a diamond ; but the diamond, if there be any, is by no means of the firft water, and indeed tolerably opaque." Thus it is, that all nations, when put in the balance by the fteady hand of a prejudiced Englifhman, are found too light ; and hence proceeds the remarkable cold-

nefs

nefs and indifference they all evince toward a foreigner on their firſt acquaintance.

The French in their own eſtimation are the only
thinking beings in the univerſe. They vouchſafe
ſometimes to converſe with ſtrangers; but it is, as
creatures of a ſuperior nature may be conceived to
converſe with men, who of courſe derive the greateſt emolument and importance from ſuch conde-
ſcenſion.   Such among them are peculiarly diſguſt-
ing, who with pretended compaſſion, and an hateful diſplay of nice equity, deign to allow a few
grains of genius or virtue to other nations; although
it very plainly appears, that this favourable opinion is not given to their merits; but is a ſponta-
neous effuſion of the exuberant politeneſs in theſe
moſt courteous people.   Theſe men ſurely will not
have the effrontery to deny, that they look upon all
nations who do not equal the French in power, or
who are ſomewhat beneath them in ſmartneſs, or
in a taſte for the frivolous arts, that are the ſtudy and
the glory of Frenchmen, as barbarians, and deſpiſe
them accordingly.   Their geſtures, converſations,
and writings, daily betray their firm perſuaſion,
that there is nothing great, noble, or amiable out
of their empire, and that nothing perfect can be
produced any where elſe, but under the foſtering
patronage of their *grand Monarque*.

, The

The French think themſelves entitled to give laws to every nation, becauſe all Europe implicitly follow the dictates of their milliners, taylors, hair-dreſſers, and cooks. Where is the Frenchman who will deny, that his countrymen think themſelves the firſt and greateſt people of the globe? How ill can Mr. Lefranc, in one of the diſcourſes he addreſſes to the king, brook the audacity of the Engliſh, who dare to put themſelves on a level with the French; for Patin himſelf has ſaid, " That the Britons were among men, what wolves are among 'the qua-drupeds?" How many numberleſs times have not the French ſtiled their ſovereign, the firſt monarch of the world? Eſteeming themſelves the firſt-born ſons of nature, they will ſometimes deign to look on their neighbours as their younger brethren, and will allow them to be laborious, tolerably good collectors, or epitomizers; nay, occaſionally, men of penetration. But why is Newton deſpiſed in France for his uſeful diſcoveries, becauſe he did not eſpy all things? Why is Raphael himſelf called ſo poor and ſpiritleſs, and his divine picture of the transfiguration weak and lifeleſs? Innumerable in-ſtances of that national pride, which allows no great men out of France, are too well known not to be the ridicule of other nations. The French repeatedly prefer their ſuperficial trifler, Boileau, to the harmoni-ous verſification, the ſolid and ethic reaſoning, and the glowing unfading tints, with which Pope has de-

D 4 , lineated

lineated the nature, foibles, and frailties of mankind.
And let us only recollect, that it is a truth in the hiftory of the progrefs of genius, that at the fame time
that Italy poffeffed the moft inimitable poets and
actors, and that Shakefpeare, the bright morning
ftar of the drama, broke forth in England, France
could boaft of none but the moft wretched rhy-
mers.

Upon the whole, vanity and felf-conceit are equally predominant in all nations. The Greenlander,
who laps with his dog in the fame platter, defpifes
the invaders of his country, the Danes. The Cof-
facks and Calmucks poffefs the greateft contempt
for their mafters, the Ruffians. The Negroes too,
though the moft ftupid among the inhabitants of
the earth, are exceffively vain. Afk the Caribbee Indians, who live at the mouth of the Oronoque, from
what nation they derive their origin ; they anfwer,
" why, we only are men." In fhort, there is hardly
any nation under the fun, in which inftances of
pride, vanity, and arrogance, do not occur. They all,
more or lefs, refemble the Canadian, who thinks he
compliments an European, when he fays, " He is a
man as well as I :" or the Spanifh preacher, who, dif-
courfing upon the temptation of Jefus by the devil,
enthufiaftically exclaimed, " But happily for mankind, and fortunately for the Son of God, the lofty
tops of the Pyrennees hid the delightful country
of

of Spain from the eyes of the Redeemer, or the temptation had affuredly been too ftrong for our bleffed Lord !"

Each nation, too, fafhions its ideas of beauty or deformity by the refemblance or difference it perceives between itfelf and others. The Indian fabulifts recount, that there is in thofe regions a country, all the inhabitants of which are hump-backed. A well-fhaped youth happened to vifit this traft, whom the honeft crookbacks no fooner faw, than they gathered round him to fee the monftrous deformity of the ftranger's figure, their aftonifhment at which was vifible in every countenance, extending its effects even to the extremities of their hunches, and the ridicule it occafioned burft forth in loud fits of laughter and derifion. As the youth's good luck would have it, there was a wife man among this gibbous fraternity, who perhaps had before feen fuch a *lufus naturæ* as ftraight-fhouldered men ; he addreffed the multitude as follows: " My good friends, what are you about ? let us not infult the unfortunate. Heaven created us well made and beautiful, and adorned our backs with graceful protuberances ; let us then rather repair to the temple, and give thanks to the Eternal for thefe ineftimable bleffings."

Whoever, therefore, would not in his own country be efteemed a foreigner, or who would not incur

the

the general contempt of the intellectually deformed society in which he lives, muſt hold the ſame opinions as are held around him, muſt fall in with all the reigning prejudices, and muſt, as much as poſ-ſible, bow his back to the faſhion of the national humour; for if he ſhould have the humility to think meanly, however deſervingly ſo, of his country or its manners, he will be reckoned an unnatural calumniator.

CHAPTER THE FOURTH.

OF PRIDE ARISING IN NATIONS FROM IMAGINARY ADVANTAGES.

THE various appearances of national pride all converge to two diftinct genera, each of them fub-divifible into feveral fpecies. The advantages on which national pride is founded, are either imagi-nary or real, which diftinction forms the grand dif-ference between the two original kinds of pride; both of them are difcoverablei n the moft confider-able nations, for every one has its prejudices, which are the foundation of its particular vanity: its pride, however, is often grounded on a true and juft conception of its own advantages; and in this cafe it is materially different from that refulting from prejudices: and, on the other hand, the pride arifing from imaginary advantages is ever, more than the other fort, fure to appear in an over-bearing fenfe of pre-eminence and contempt for others.

Self-conceit often makes men think they per-ceive advantages where none exift, or attribute qua-lifications to themfelves, in which they are evidently deficient.

3

deficient. , Our vanity is never more pleafed than when our imperfections are gloffed over, except when they are even exalted into the very contrary advantages by the delufive power of adulation. Proceeding on this principle, a poet once ventured to compare the ftature of a lady of high rank, who had no other perfonal defect than being very diminutive, to the towering cedar : the little creature, on hearing the author recite his verfes, could not control the lively fenfations his flattery excited, but fat fmiling on her chair. "Go no further," faid a byftander to the poet, whofe fimile of the cedar recurred every moment; "go no further, for fear the good lady in the heat of her happinefs fhould ftart up, and at once difcover her natural defect and thy abominable deception."

Self-conceit builds on imaginary advantages or perfections the moft ridiculous pride ; like that with which a Spaniard or a Portuguefe ftruts, when he compares his nut-brown complexion with the fwarthy hide of a Moor ; or which puffs into confequence a burgher of Bern, when he can fill his belly to the utmoft. The inhabitants of the Ladrones believe, that their language is the only one in the world, and therefore that all the other nations of the earth are dumb. An Indian tribe on the banks of the Ohio in North America have hair of an extraordinary length ; they therefore fuppofe all people

with

with fhort hair are flaves. The Turks, who are
reproached for the inconfiftency with which they
diftribute offices and places to fuch as cannot be
fuppofed to have the proper qualification for filling
them; when, for inftance, they are accufed with
having put a toll-gatherer at the head of an army;
reply with the greateft indignation, "That a Turk
is fit for every thing:" nay, fultan Ofman once made
one of his gardeners viceroy of Cyprus, becaufe he
had feen him plant out cabbages in a particular clever
manner. When the Ruffian general, Apraxin, was up-
braided with having fuffered himfelf to be furprized
by Marfhal Lehwald, he coolly rejoined, "The Ruffians never employ either fcouts or fpies." An in-
habitant of the province of Maine in France, proud
of the temperate genial warmth with which his
native country is bleffed, has lately produced a
phyfical hiftory of climates, according to the tafte
of the old fchools, in which he praifes the inhabitants of the warmer, and depreciates thofe of the
colder countries; of courfe, giving the preference
in every thing good and great to the happy tem-
perature refulting from the middle fituation in
which he places his native land. To this blefied
region belong Upper Germany, part of Spain, the
civilized countries of Wallachia and Moldavia, and
the humane and peaceful inhabitants of the frontiers of the Auftrian and Turkifh empires; together
with

with the Coſſacks, Calmucks, Afghans, and other people equally celebrated for knowledge and fentiment.

Self-conceit towers to ſuch an amazing height, and has withal ſo narrow a baſis, that it is very eaſily overthrown, and its evident futility is often too great to require a refutation. Heartily welcome, therefore, for my part, are the Myrmidons who aſſiſted at the ſiege of Troy, to the ſatisfaction of knowing that they were deſcended from induſtrious ants; and the kings of Madura, to the honour of deriving their pedigree, in a right line, from a jack aſs, on which account they always treat every long-eared brayer as a brother, and never fail when it rains to hold an umbrella over him, which they would not on any account do to his driver, as that would be a derogation of their dignity, for he is not a branch of their highly illuſtrious houſe. I cannot but ſmile at the national vanity of many among the French, who even yet trumpet forth the conqueſt of Mahon, when the whole world knows that this reduction of a ſmall garriſon, left entirely to its own exertions, and deſtitute of ſuccour, was followed by a war pregnant with diſaſters to France, which ſeverely ſmarted in every quarter of the globe *.

* This ſentence the French tranſlator has omitted.

I read

I read with the fame fenfations, the before-mentioned French author of the phyfical hiftory of climates revile the northern nations. "They, to be fure, have invented the moft fenfelefs forms of government that ever exifted, namely, the Englifh, and its attendant, liberty; from them proceeds the practice of duelling; while, forfooth, murder and affaffination are more manly, for they are more practifed in the favoured warmer regions: in fhort, thofe who live beyond a certain degree of latitude deferve the loweft rank among men." This is certainly highly ridiculous. Nor does the vanity of the Italians more move my fpleen, who call the Germans downright blockheads, becaufe they do not know how to prepare any other poifons than can be counteracted by the phyfical art, or which appear in manifold fymptoms; fuch as the inflammation of the throat, the ftomach, or the inteftines, or the difcoloration and incruftation of the fkin; while, on the contrary, the cunning Italian can kill with poifons infinitely more powerful, fubtle, and irremediable. It is impoffible to recount all the imaginary advantages from which national pride, in its widely extended field of exiftence, is or has been derived: I fhall only touch upon fuch as are moft prominent; and by particularizing them, reflect as much glory on the nation to which thefe appertain, as a French general does, when he drags

along

along with him into the field two thoufand * cooks,
and efteems it due to his confequence and fame to
have a hundred difhes ferved up at his table.

* The French tranflator has " twenty," and inftead of a
hundred difhes, has " plates for a hundred guefts." We fhall
have many other occafions to remark the wilful errors into
which this national Frenchman has fallen; hoping that we ourfelves, in every refpect, have done juftice to the original from
which it is tranflated.

CHAPTER THE FIFTH.

OF THE PRIDE ARISING FROM THE IMAGINARY ANTIQUITY OR NOBILITY OF A NATION.

THE vanity of mankind has ever filled the immenſe vacuity beyond the authentic memorials of the origin of every nation, with fabulous hiſtory ; at pleaſure removing their antiquity to the remoteſt ages, in order proportionally to increaſe its luſtre. Whatever an itinerant bard ſung, or an orator raved, became frequently an univerſal tradition, and in proceſs of time almoſt an article of religion. The probability of theſe flattering inventions could no more be called in queſtion, when revered ages had ſanctioned the opinion. A prodigy of antient times becomes too eaſily, in the eyes of purblind poſterity, an undeniable truth, while the remoteneſs of the age precludes a proper ſearch by which to diſtinguiſh falſehood from probability, and this again from certainty ; and we are ever more averſe to attempt theſe diſquiſitions, if pride find its account in the well-invented fiction.

The ſuperlatively intelligent and ſuperlatively grandiloquous Athenians conceived they had ſprung

E   up,

up, like mufhrooms, from the Attic foil, and therefore cherifhed the moft fovereign contempt for
colonies. The Arcadians rejected with contemp-
tuous difdain the fcience of aftrology, becaufe they
believed themfelves antecedent to the moon. The
Egyptians were perfuaded they were the moft ancient inhabitants of the earth : according to their
chronology, their empire exifted forty-eight thoufand
eight hundred and fixty-three years before the age
of Alexander ; it was firft peopled by gods who were
hatched from eggs, then by demi-gods, and laftly
by men.

The Japanefe in the fame manner fuppofe themfelves to be lineally defcended from gods. They are
much offended when their origin is deduced from
the Chinefe, or any other oriental nation ; but they
have, neverthelefs, the modefty to fix the commencement of thefe gods, and do not entirely veil
them in the darknefs of eternity.

Kuni-Toko-Dat-Sii-No-Mikotto, the firft deity
who arofe from Chaos, fixed his refidence in Japan,
which he created prior to all other countries : this
divinity, with his fix fucceffors, form the dynafty
of heavenly fpirits who took Japan under their particular protection, the duration of which is ftated
to be an innumerable feries of ages. The three firft
of thefe gods had no wives, but impregnated themfelves,

felves, and brought forth what they had begotten. The four laft provided themfelves with women, yet propagated one another in a fupernatural way; till Ifanagi-No-Mikotto learnt of the bird Ifiatadakki, our by no means contemptible method of gene‑ ration; but the line of heavenly intelligences in Japan was hereby broken and put an end to, for the race of the Ifanagi loft its divine nature by this carnal innovation.

Ifanagi was tranflated, like his predeceffors, from earth to heaven; and his fon Tenfio-Dai-Dfin, who is the fame with the fun, commenced the dynafty of the five demi-gods, or gods incarnate, who, according to the chronology of the Japanefe, reigned in all, without interruption, for the fpace of two millions, three hundred, forty-two thoufand, four hundred, and fixty-feven, years; from thefe it is pretended that the whole nation defcends, without exception; and the great pre-eminence of their Dairo arifes from his being reputed the offspring of the eldeft fon of the firft demi-god. The hiftory of this dynafty of god-men is preferved in the archives of the prieft of the Sinto; and exceeds, in puerile tales and romantic fictions, all that ever the moft extra‑ vagant imagination engendered. In many towns and villages in Japan, memorials of thefe heroes are fhewn; and their armour is hung up in their temples for the edification and adoration of the multitude.

China

China is exceffively vain of the numerous centuries its monarchy is fuppofed to have fubfifted.
The voluminous hiftory of this empire begins, according to du Halde, with the reign of the emperor
Fo-Hi, who muft have lived about two thoufand
five hundred years before the birth of Chrift, at a
time when the Affyrians were poffeffed of a feries of
aftronomical obfervations. Notwithftanding the
obfcurity of this origin, the Chinefe chronology
defcends from the reign of Yao in an uninterrupted
fucceffion of twenty-two dynafties to our times :
fome of them even carry back the commencement
of their empire to an æra far beyond the creation of
the world. But this whole account, copied by father du Halde from Chinefe fuperftition, and though,
for well-known reafons, fupported by Voltaire, has
been wholly overthrown by a very learned Tartar, a
man free from all Chinefe prejudices, Nyen-Hy-Jao,
viceroy of Canton, and with it its vaft fuperftruc-
ture of vanity and pride.

The inhabitants of Indoftan penetrate ftill deeper
into the fabulous world. Bernier made many enquiries of the learned men at Benares, a city on the
Ganges, which he calls the Athens of India, about
their chronology ; they immediately and readily
counted millions of years on their fingers to him,
in order to mark their remote origin; and the antiquity of their Sanfcrit, or the language of the
learned,

learned, in which their God revealed his will to them through Brama, was fixed at many thoufands of years.

The hiftory of the Malabars extends to an infinite time: they will tell you of Darma, of Schoren, of Pandyen, and of many other kings, who muft have lived long before the beginning of the world according to our computation : but you muft not afk them the names of princes who reigned only three hundred years ago, for of them they are totally ignorant.

The yet uncivilized inhabitants of Paraguay give to the moon the endearing appellation of mother ; and when their parent is eclipfed, they run out of their huts with the greateft activity, and making the moft hideous lamentations, they fhoot a vaft number of arrows into the air in order to defend the moon from the dogs who attack her, and want to tear her in pieces, which they take to be the caufe of the obfcuration of that luminary, and the fhooting continues till it refumes its wonted brightnefs.

The Swedes have a long table of kings, in an uninterrupted chain of fucceffion from Noah down to his prefent Majefty. The Edda and Wolufpo are, next to the holy Scriptures, efteemed the moft valuable monuments of antiquity by every one who

is

is a true Swede. Rudbeck, more concerned for the imaginary honour of his country than for hiſtoric truth, gives the Swediſh monarchy a duration of twenty centuries before the birth of Chriſt: whereas Rabenius expreſſes his doubts whether Sweden was even peopled ſo late as the beginning of the fifth century; and that, even according to Dalin's hypotheſis, Sweden only emerged from the ocean about four hundred years before our æra. The Laplanders derive their origin immediately from a god, who produced at the ſame time both their anceſtor, and the anceſtor of the Swedes; but the latter in a violent thunder-ſtorm crept under a tree for ſhelter, while the courageous progenitor of the Laplanders remained inflexible and intrepid, expoſed to the whole force of the tempeſt under the ſcowling brow of heaven.

The pride which ariſes from the imaginary nobility of a nation, flows from the ſame ſource with that founded on antiquity, for we always think our nobility more antient the leſs we are acquainted with its real age.

Nobility is, in reality, great and honourable, when it is built on our own merit, or upon the exalted virtues and tranſcendent actions of our anceſtors; but the pride of nobility is ridiculous and abſurd, when one only glories in a title or a coat of arms,

and

and prefumes fo much on the deferts of one's forefathers, as to conceive that the acquifition of perfonal efteem can be difpenfed with. A noble birth,
when accompanied by a weak underftanding, produces in the right honourable owner nought but
arrogance; and felf-conceit becomes noblemen who
have the honour to be defcended from heroes, and
the misfortune to be diffimilar in every thing to the
worthy founders of their race, as little as family
pride does the man who boafts of the noble blood
that runs in his veins, while he is without a pair
of breeches.

In Spain, every farmer and every tradefman has
his genealogical tables, which begin generally, as
thofe of Welchmen do, at Noah's ark. This
imaginary anceftry forbids a Spanifh countryman to
plough his own ground; labour is, in his opinion,
only fit for flaves; and the man who works two hours
during the day, is of greater confideration and more
noble blood, than he who employs fix out of the
twenty-four in ufeful occupation: he therefore gets
a foreigner to take off his hands the agricultural
part, and at the fame time the profits arifing from it,
while he lounges at home thrumming over a tink-
ling guitar. But when fuch an illuftrious peafant
debafes himfelf fo far as to hold the plough, he yet
knows how to give an air of grandeur to this mean
employment; he fticks a couple of cocks' feathers

in

in his hat, and has his cloak and fword lying be-
fide him, fo that as foon as he perceives a traveller
or a ftranger, he inftantly abandons the plough,
throws the cloak over his fhoulders, claps on his
toledo, ftrokes his muftachios, and ftruts over the
field with the appearance of a cavalier taking the
air. The common people in Spain think the French
all beggars, becaufe there is many a Frenchman
who earns a livelihood there by manual labour :
the Swifs will foon have the fame reputation, for
with heartfelt concern, even while now writing, I
fee whole droves of honeft, fturdy, Roman Catholic
Switzers, with their buxom wives and numerous
children, pafs by my windows in their way to Spain,
to avoid, as they themfelves fay, ftarving at home.

The Florentine nobleffe are uncommonly referved and haughty towards ftrangers, who cannot
prove their nobility, and may, perchance, be mere
tradefmen ; yet it is an acknowledged fact, that there
is a little window towards the ftreet in every palace
or large houfe in Florence, with an iron knocker
and an empty flafk hung over it, as a fign, that
wine is to be fold there by the bottle. It is not
thought inconfiftent for a Florentine nobleman to
fell a pound of figs, or half a yard of ribbon, or
to take money for a bottle of four wine ; yet it
would be a difparagement to his nobility, if he were
to introduce a meritorious, but untitled Englifhman,
into

into a public company where every one, however insignificant otherwise, who is of any tolerable family, inherits, or assumes the title of prince, count, or marquis.

At Verona, the person who conducts strangers to visit what is worthy of remark in that city, is a decayed nobleman of one of the first families of the place. When one of my friends entered with this man into a coffee-house, he found his conductor was addressed, by his brother nobles, by the title of Excellence : such Eccellenza's abound in the public places of Naples, where they walk about in worn-out gold waistcoats, with well darned stockings.

In the mountains of Piedmont, and in the county of Nice, there are some representatives of very ancient and noble families, reduced to the condition of common peasants ; but they still retain the ancient pride of their houses, and boast of the noble blood that runs in their veins. A gentleman, in travelling through these mountains, was obliged to pass the night in the cottage of one of these rusticated nobles, who called to his son in the evening, " *Chevalier, a tu donné à manger aux cochons ?*"

The nobles of the nation of the Natches, in Louisiania, stile the common people *Miche Miche Quipi*, which mean, stinkards ; they themselves are,

in

in different ranks, funs, noblemen, and honourable
gentlemen : the funs are fuch as are defcended from
a man and woman, who pretended to have immediately iffued from the fun; this man and woman
became lawgivers to the Natches, from the com-
monality of whom they ordained that their race
fhould for ever be feparated. · In order, however,
to prevent their blood being adulterated by any
mixture with that of the lower ranks, and to provide againft the flippery conduct of their wives,
they enacted, that nobility fhould only defcend in
the female line. Their children, both male and
female, were ftiled funs, and refpected as fuch, but
with this diftinction, that in the males this privilege
appertained only to one man, and became extinct
at his death; the females were all born funs, and
their male offspring are funs equally with their
mothers, but the iffue of thefe are not funs, but
noblemen; their grandfons, honourable gentlemen;
and their great grandfons, ftinkards.

National pride, founded on imaginary antiquity,
is, therefore, a great folly; which, however, many
enlightened nations give into, and which pleafes
them as much, as a genealogical parchment does a
country gentleman, who, filled with ham and peafe,
plumes himfelf on his long line of anceftors.

CHAPTER THE SIXTH.

OF RELIGIOUS PRIDE.

T RUE and falfe religion has ever been, among all nations, in narrow minds, an object of a particular pride, which foon becomes a branch of national pride : a bigot not only accounts his religion the only true one, but hates and defpifes every other, and pronounces fentence of eternal damnation on all who do not think, in this refpect, exactly as he does.

Religious pride confifts in the prepoffeffion we entertain of the infallibility of our religion, and the idea that it is the only one conducting to falvation; in confequence whereof the followers of every other doctrine are pofitively no other than fteaks ready prepared for the devil's gridiron. A religion need not at all be true to lead its followers to this point, for falfities are embraced with no lefs obftinacy than truths. But let the religion on which you pride yourfelf proceed immediately from the gofpel of Jefus and his Apoftles, and be of courfe true; yet to condemn others who have not had the fame op- portunity of receiving inftruction, or who have not

the

the capacity to comprehend a fyftem of religion which is diametrically oppofite to all they have feen, heard, or been taught from their earlieft youth, is, in my opinion, utter infanity.

Men ought not to pronounce fo lightly on each other. The fame God of love and charity will judge us all, and he will judge us according to the integrity and fincerity with which we fhall have ferved him. If every one does not exactly take the neareft and beft path, he is notwithftanding in a road that leads to the fame end, which he will undoubtedly attain if he believes in revelation ; whereby we are all taught to pafs a virtuous and unfpotted life, by which we become partakers of all the promifes of religion. The hope of falvation is grounded on the moral character of a man, and not on his theology ; not fo much on his opinions and his knowledge, as on the worthinefs, purity, and honefty of his life. In all religions, therefore, we may be really pious, if we habituate ourfelves to the examination and purification of our hearts and conduct, and make the honour and fervice of that God whom we acknowledge, the chief motive of all our ferious actions *.

* The French translator in a note condemns this whole paffage, and declares, " That none can be faved but Catholics, as is proved in a multitude of excellent works."

That

That felf-deception and prejudices, however, are no where fo glaringly violent, as in religious matters; has been moft juftly a caufe of univerfal complaint. Priefts, of all religions, have ever vociferated to their followers over the whole world, " We only are in the right ; it is our religion only that is the true one, and all others confift of nothing but the greateft abfurdities, and the moft abominable doctrines." Even in the church of love, gentlenefs, and long-fuffering, every party and every fect anathematize the doctrine which differs but a hair's breadth from their own. One fyftem refutes the theology maintained and afferted by another fyftem, and each difproves what the other affirms. There is fcarcely any error that is not defended by one fect or other as an undoubted truth. Each party glories in its proofs, and derides its antagonifts moft triumphantly; each writes and affirms as if it were infallible, though they write and affirm the moft contrary tenets ; as the force of their arguments is derived from the country in which they are adduced; for what in one place is accounted a divine truth, is twenty miles off efteemed a moft palpable falfehood.

All this appears to me the lefs extraordinary, as, according to the teftimony of unprejudiced church hiftorians, the fpirit of party, of prepoffeffion, and the opinion entertained of the fanctity and infallibility of the particular doctrine they adhere to, often

fo

fo much dazzles divines of great erudition and penetration, that they overlook common fenfe in defend-
ing their opinions.   It has often with the jufteft concern been obferved, that difputes are continually entertained without foundation, and that the Bible is
proved from a polemic fyftem, inftead of the fyftem
being proved from the Bible ; that the Scriptures are
often only known by the paffages and quotations
which have been adduced to confirm a certain profeffion of faith by the teachers of that profeffion, in their
fermons and writings ; and when they have faid fuch
and fuch words occur in fuch a particular part of
the Bible, it has been implicitly believed, nay, the
quotation has been read in exactly the fame expreffions, or the leaders of religious parties have dif-
torted and mutilated the paffages, taken words ab-
ftractedly, and without their connection, fo that
they have been wrefted from their original meaning ;
and, when by torturing them, in every fenfe, with
the moft pitiful fophiftry, they have at length adapted them to their own peculiar interpretation, immediately each party has fet up a loud *te deum* for
their imaginary victory.

And it is from fuch oracles, as from the pureft
fprings, that moft Chriftians feek to be informed of
eternal truth ; and thereby they only increafe the
bigotry and zeal which has been inftilled into them,
in their earlieft youth, by their inconfiderate teachers:

whatever

whatever they have been taught to look upon as holy, inviolable truths, always remain fo ; they find proofs where there are abfolutely none, and hold the principles of their opponents to be futile and ungrounded, nay irreligious and profane, before they have ever examined them. By this unreafon-ablenefs of both fides their animofity increafes, and combatants and controverfies, errors, herefies, here-tics, and heretic revilers, multiply *ad infinitum.*

All fects and religious parties have accordingly conceived themfelves infallible ; each entertains the miferable opinion, that among all the many religious communities, theirs alone poffefs the knowledge of divine truth in its purity, without confidering that, in fome points, others may be nearer the truth than themfelves. They reciprocally contemn, abhor, and reproach each other with blindnefs, obftinacy, hardnefs of heart, or deceit ; they all believe them-felves in the ftraight road to Heaven, and that all others are wandering in the path that leads to hell and perdition ; they all call upon the teftimony of one omnifcient God, which when it comes to be narrowly looked into, proves to be no other than the teftimony of their own fect. Every man of confined underftanding prides himfelf on his re-ceived opinions, and looks upon all who do not agree with him in religious principles, as impure and defpicable ; fo that to revile another fyftem of

religion,

religion, always implies the praife of our own; for it ever is, in this refpect, as with our watches; we all depend on the truth of the one we poffefs, which alone points out the exact time of the day, while all others go either too flow or too faft.

This conceit of the excellency of religious opinions is often carried fo far, that all great men are held to belong to our own perfuafion. The Turks are morally convinced that Adam, Noah, Mofes, the Prophets, nay, Chrift himfelf, were all good Mahometans ; and according to the Alkoran, Abraham was neither a Jew nor a Chriftian, but a true believing Muffulman. In Voltaire's opinion, Fenelon is a deift. In that of the peafants in the neighbourhood of Naples, Virgil was a faint; and a little edifice near his grave, a chapel where he ufed to read mafs.

On the other hand, a contempt for a different religion is often occafioned or increafed by the obfcurity and mifconception of its rites and tenets. Tacitus fays, that the Jews adore, in their holy of holies, the image of an afs; becaufe an animal of that fpecies had been their guide in the wildernefs, when they had loft their way, and had brought them to frefh water when they were perifhing with thirft. Plutarch relates, that the Jews pay divine honours to fwine; becaufe thefe creatures had taught them

them husbandry.; that their feast of the tabernacles
is celebrated in honour of Bacchus, and their fab-
bath inftituted for the like purpofe. The cuftoms
of the very beft among men, the primitive Chriftians, either mifunderftood, or wholly unknown,
became handles for the moft fenfelefs contempt and
the moft cruel perfecution : the Jews alleged they
were guilty of the fouleft crimes; the Heathens
affirmed, that an afs, with eagle's talons, was the
object of their adoration; that a new born in-
fant, entirely covered over with confecrated flour,
was prefented, like fome myftic fymbol of initiation,
to the knife of the profelyte, who, unknowingly,
inflicted many a fecret wound on the innocent victim of his error; that as foon as the cruel deed
was perpetrated, the fectaries drank up the blood,
greedily tore afunder the quivering members, and
pledged themfelves to eternal fecrecy, by a mutual
confcioufnefs of guilt. It was as confidently aver-
red, that this inhuman facrifice was fucceeded by
a fuitable entertainment, in which intemperance
ferved as a provocative to brutal luft; till at the appointed moment the lights were extinguifhed, fhame
was banifhed, nature was forgotten, and, as accident might direct, the darknefs of the night was
polluted by the inceftuous commerce of fifters and
brothers, of mothers and of fons; it was afferted
that they threatened to involve in a general con-
flagration the whole earth, and all the heavenly

bodies, by means of their infernal magic : in fine,
that they were murderers, adulterers, committers
of inceft, and enemies of the gods, of the emperor,
of chaftity, and of human nature.

It too often happens, that the revilers of a religion, are not acquainted with it, becaufe they hate
it; and, *vice verfa*, that they hate it, becaufe they
are unacquainted with it: they attribute to its profeffors doctrines which, perhaps, they abhor, and inftitutions of which they never once had an idea:
they fcatter the moft contradictory and abfurd ca-
lumnies againft the followers of an oppofite creed,
as we have already proved by many inftances; to
which I fhall add but one more. A Franconian
catholic of quality believed that his fon, a very intelligent young man, was infected with the principles of Proteftantifm, as he was particularly inqui-
fitive and ftudious; as an antidote to this fuppofed
venom, the right honourable, free, and imperial
fool, hit upon the following precept, which he fo-
lemnly charged his fon to obferve, as he was fetting
out on his travels; " Take care, my fon," fays he,
" to avoid the company of Proteftant divines, for
they are all fodomites."

A people, who conceive they alone profefs the
true religion, will not only believe themfelves under
the immediate protection, and objects of the pecu-

liar

liar favour of the Supreme Being, but will exprefs.
the moft ill-natured abhorrence for the followers of
another religion, whom they even do not treat with
common humanity. The Ifraelites always looked
upon themfelves as the Lord's anointed people; and,
in the time of our Saviour, they accounted the Sa-
maritans unworthy of their regard or converfation;
their Rabbins held it an unlawful and indecorous
thing, either to requeft a favour of a Samaritan, or
to accept of any civility from one of that fect.
Even to this day the Jews refufe to receive any wine
from Chriftians, for fear the errors and vices of
Chriftianity fhould be infufed together with the
liquor into their Hebraic purity. According to the
precepts of the Talmud, no Jew muft falute a Chriftian without inwardly curfing him, nor wifh him a
good journey without a fecret tacit addition, like
that of Pharaoh to the Red Sea, or of Haman to the
gallows.

The Mahometan religion is excellently adapted.
to inftil into its followers the greateft arrogance.
Mahomet, their holy prophet, is, according to the
Turks, the man whom God and his angels daily
converfed with; to whom the ftars paid obeifance;
whom the trees and ftones advanced to greet;
who fplit the moon with his finger; who made
roafted fhoulders of veal to fpeak; the apoftle
of the Lord, who in the twelfth year of his divine

miffion

miffion was taken up into heaven, and was taught the fecrets of Omnipotence from the mouth of Omnipotence itfelf; add to this, the promifes made by Mahomet, to all his followers, of the future fplendour of his empire in this world, and the voluptuoufnefs and magnificence of it in the next: hence it naturally follows, that a Turk entertains a fovereign contempt for all other humbler fyftems of religion.

The Turks, far removed from connecting themfelves with the followers of Ali, apply to them the moft opprobrious epithets; they call themfelves *Sunni*, or true believers; but thefe they ftile *Schias*, which is as much as to fay, a defpicable and reprobate fect. A Turk very feldom will affirm a notorious falfehood; wherefore, whenever any proof is required of what he relates, his general anfwer is, "Doft thou think I am a Chriftian?" All who are not true believers are, in the eyes of the Turks, fo many dogs, whofe very approach would defile an orthodox Muffulman; on which account, no infidel is allowed to enter a certain tract of land fituated between Mecca and Medina, which is fo exceedingly holy, and the regulation which forbids its entrance to any but true believers fo ftrictly obferved, that fhould the ambaffador or legate of any infidel prince, on his journey to Mecca, fet his foot on this confecrated earth, the Xerif is obliged, by his office, to interdict him from advancing, and

to

to order him to retire, and if he is not fcared away by thefe menaces, to ufe violence. No Chriftian is allowed to refide in the whole of the country of Hejaz in Arabia, becaufe the holy cities of Mecca and Medina are fituated there. Neither Jews nor Chriftians are allowed in Egypt to be prefent at the opening of the canals of the Nile, left the water fhould be kept back by their uncleannefs. ;

In the bofom of Mahometanifm too, as well as in the Chriftian religion, the feveral fects accufe and re-vile each other, that they have falfified and perverted the doctrine of their prophet, by which the mutual hatred of the people is nurtured, and the idea of toleration exploded. The Perfians annually cele-brate a feftival in honour of their prophet Ali, in which two oxen are exhibited; the one, which they take care to be the ftrongeft, is called Ali, and the other, always very inferior in ftrength to his anta-gonift, Omar; thefe are made to fight, and as Ali always obtains the victory, the fpectators from thence conclude that they alone are orthodox Mahometans, and the Turks hereticks. The Turks, on the other hand, maintain that the Perfians are the identical faddle-affes on which the Jews are to canter away to hell at the day of judgment.

As the Mahometans are unjuft towards the Chrif-tians, fo the latter are equally unjuft towards the former.

former. No Turk ever entertained the leaſt doubt, or attempted to ſpeak ill of the unity of the God-head; and yet they havė very often in Chriſtendom been called idolaters and worſhippers of the ſtars; while they are ſuch ſtrenuous advocates for one God, that miſunderſtanding one of our fundamental doctrines, they upbraid us with polytheiſm; and yet they have in many Chriſtian books been ſtiled Pagans, and their empire Paganiſm.

The Arab, in the conviction that his caliph is infallible, laughs at the ſtupid credulity of the Tar-tar, who holds his Lama to be immortal. A feather, a horn, a ſhell, the claw of a lobſter, a root, or any thing elſe that has been conſecrated by a few unintelligible words, is an object of adoration to the negroes, and the ſolemn prototype on which they take their oaths: they find in the earth they tread on an immenſe number of gods, and ridicule the Europeans for their poverty in this reſpect. Thoſe who inhabit mount Bata believe, that whoever de-vours a roaſted cuckow before his death is a ſaint; and, firmly perſuaded of the infallibility of this mode of ſanctification, deride the Indians, who drag a cow to the bed of a dying perſon, and pinching her tail, are ſure, if by that method they can make the crea-ture void her urine in the face of the patient, he is immediately tranſlated into the third heaven; they ſcoff at the ſuperſtition of the Tartarian princes who

think

think their beatification fecured, provided they can eat of the holy excrements of their Lama ; and they ridicule the Bramins, who, for the better purification of their new converts, require them to eat cow dung for the fpace of fix months ; while thefe would, one and all, in their turn, if they were told the cuckow-method of falvation, as heartily de-fpife and laugh at it.

In the kingdom of Tanjore there are Bramins, who, deriving their origin from their god Brama, hold themfelves fuperior to all earthly power ; they are fo very holy, that the bare touch of one of an inferior caft, a Parea, would defile them ; nay, the latter muft not prefume to worfhip the fame deities. Thefe Bramins can in no cafe be punifhed with death, and are in poffeffion of fo many, and fuch extraordinary privileges, that they rule without controul or oppofition over the lower claffes of the inhabitants of Malabar, who quietly fubmit to the mandates of thefe inflated and indolent priefts.

In Japan, the devotees of the fect of Insja-Fufe, had the fame ridiculous idea of their own immaculate fanctity, and retreated with abhorrence from any communication with other men. The priefts of the Sinto, or primeval religion of Japan, are equally infected with the pride of this tranfcendent holinefs, and avoid, with the utmoft haughtinefs,

both

both the laity and the clergy profeſſing the Budſo, or new religion of Japan, whom they take great care to hold no correſpondence with, which would be the loweſt degradation of their dignity ; while the natural reciprocal contempt of the Budſo divines for thoſe of the Sinto, is by no means inferior.

The Dairo, or pope of Japan, is reſpected almoſt as a god in his life-time : the earth is not worthy the touch of his feet, and the ſun is not allowed the favour of ſhining on his head ; the holineſs of his hair, his beard, and his nails, is ſo great, that to cut off or pare them is not permitted except during his ſleep ; for the Japaneſe believe, that all that which the body of their Dairo then loſes is only ſtolen from him, and that ſuch a robbery is by no means ſo ſacrilegious as to take them from him while awake, for that would argue in him a too near ap-p · ɔach to mortality.   In former times the Dairo was obliged to ſit a few hours every morning on his throne, like a ſtatue, without moving his hands, his feet, his head, his eyes, or any part of his body, in order that the empire might enjoy the moſt profound tranquillity ; peſtilence, famine, or war, would, agreeable to the opinion then entertained, immediately have afflicted that unlucky province to-wards which the Dairo had caſt a look. The firſt who was properly emperor of Japan, was ſtiled the man of ſublime extraction, the prince of heaven, the ſon

of

of the gods; and thefe titles have remained to the
Dairo, who on his death enjoys, in common with
the Roman emperors, the honour of an apotheofis;
while the Cubofoma, or worldly fovereign of Japan,
who is the territorial lord, like the prefent kings of
France, Spain, Portugal, and Naples, contents himfelf with the more folid honours of earthly power.

The court of his Japanefe holinefs is compofed
of highly illuftrious perfonages, who though they
are not above exercifing themfelves in the manu-
facture of ftraw-bafkets, horfe-fhoes, or any other
little handicraft, to keep themfelves from ftarving;
neverthelefs, proud of their pedigree from the firft
demi-god of the fecond dynafty of Japan, they treat
the reft of mankind as dogs; nay, the dignity,
fanctity, and purity of every thing that relates to
the Dairo is fo great, that the meaneft fervant-boys
who perform the loweft offices in the temple, and
in the religious ceremonies of Japan, and whofe
ftation exactly anfwers to that of candle-fnuffer in a
play-houfe, are equally vain of their fuper-eminence
over the reft of the world. As to the univerfal
opinion entertained by the Japanefe of the Chriftians, I fhall only illuftrate the low degree of eftimation in which they are held, by the obligation they
impofed on the Dutch, to caft all their dead into
the fea, off the harbour of Nangafaki, for their
carcafes were deemed unworthy a burial in the foil
of

of Japan, although thofe lucre-loving fouls affured them they were not Chriftians, but only Hollanders.

Thus do mankind ridicule and defpife, execrate and condemn each other, becaufe each conceives himfelf to belong to the only religion which leads to falvation, or to be a being of exclufive and undefiled holinefs. The total feparation of our own, from every other religious fociety, is efteemed neceffary and indifpenfable to fanctification, and we are, therefore, never able to be impartial or equitable towards others; this feparation; the yet exifting predominant opinion in every fect of the infallibility of its own tenets; the unhappy fpirit of perfecution of many refpectable theologians; the untimely zeal, which incites us blindly to repel all attacks on the doctrines embraced by our relations and progenitors; and, above all, the great multitude of holy champions, who are continually on foot, armed at all points, ready to throw the gauntlet of defiance, and inconfiderately and unmercifully to lay about them, like the too zealous Peter, againft every one who might fhew the leaft defign of attacking the principles of their church: all this compels mankind reciprocally to abhor and condemn their fellow-creatures; becaufe one fet chufes to jog on to heaven by a different road than the other, and which, alas! is carried to fuch extravagance, that, among other inftances, a reformed clergyman, de-

tected

tected preaching his articles of belief in France, would be hanged ; and a jefuit, if caught in Sweden, would be emafculated.

Thus do we, poor miferable worms ! in our little fpan of life, prefume to hate and perfecute our brother, only becaufe we happen to differ from him in opinion refpecting an unneceffary, and nearly imperceptible refinement, or a matter that is be-yond human conception : thus do we, creatures of the duft ! arrogate the power of circumfcribing the councils of the Almighty, and prefumptuoufly dare to ftamp our paffions and prejudices, our priefts and prieftly pride, with the counterfeit image of the Lord of Heaven and of Earth.

CHAPTER THE SEVENTH.

OF NATIONAL PRIDE, AS ARISING FROM A SUPPOSED
LIBERTY, VALOUR, POWER, OR CONSIDERATION.

HERE and there we may find nations who, like
the ancient Greeks, overvalue themfelves on account
of their real freedom ; or like the modern inhabitants of Greece, treafure up the memory of the
former liberty of their country, on which they equally
pride themfelves.

The moft notorious flaves in Italy boaft of their
glorious freedom. This infatuating dream begets
a moft ludicrous elevation of mind, which is the derifion of the fubftantial republican citizen, whofe confolation does not, like that of thefe conceited flaves,
confift in mere empty founds or unmeaning words.
A citizen of San Marino knows nothing that can be
compared with ancient Rome, fave the petty· republic of which he is a member. The nobles of
Genoa, who are almoft all engaged in trade, out
of mercantile jealoufy, make ufe of the moft interefted and felfifh policy, and every kind of artifice,
to keep the coafts, which are under their dominion,
in poverty and dependance, in order that the trade

of

of the capital may not be injured; yet the poor devils at San Remo and Noli believe moſt implicitly that they are free.

Another effect of ideal liberty, is the laughable contempt and oppoſition which a conquered people have for the laws and cuſtoms of their conquerors, which, though ever ſo eligible in themſelves, it would be diſgraceful for them to adopt. The Engliſh have taken the trouble of making ſmooth, broad, and ſtraight roads both in Ireland and in Minorca, yet they have never been able to perſuade either the Iriſh or the Minorcans to uſe theſe infinitely more commodious roads in preference to their old, crooked, or miry lanes, in which, ſtupidly averſe to innovation, they continue to plunge with an elevated mien and jaded body, proud of theſe ſtill remaining veſtiges of their imaginary independence.

A third effect, reſulting from the idea of freedom, which is the chief glory of a certain great nation in Europe, is the neglect of ceremony, and the opinion that the dictates of good breeding need not be farther followed, than as they are conſiſtent with our own convenience, or our own inclinations; in conſequence of which latitude, it is no harm to throw one's ſelf back in an elbow-chair, when tired of ſitting upright; you may invite your friends to

eat

eat and drink with you at all hours, and at all fea-
fons, whether to breakfaſt, dinner, or ſupper, or
whether you have roaſt or boiled meat to give them:
you may frankly ſay the wine is good for nothing,
when it is really ſo ; and, when a lady happens in
a coach, with ſeveral gentlemen, to feel a certain
preſſing want of nature, ſhe may, conſiſtently with
the freedom of her nation, ſend for a chamber-pot
from the next houſe, and eaſe herſelf in the coach
without bluſhing *.

The pride founded upon imaginary valour, appears in an exceſſive eſtimation of our own courage,

---

* In this paſſage, which alludes to the Engliſh, Mr. Zim-
merman has fallen into a very great miſtake, for, however well
founded his aſſertions may be with reſpeƈt to the general blunt-
neſs of our charaƈter, and the little ceremony with which men
treat each other, both our regard for the fair ſex, and their
delicacy, is unimpeachable : nay, ſo far from any immodeſty
of the kind the authcr mentions being ever heard of in England, the very tale he exhibits has, in other words, been the
ſubjeƈt of ſatire among us upon the ladies of France ; and Eng-
liſhmen generally turn, with diſguſt, from the manners of
foreign females, when compared to the elegant nicety, and
delicate ſenſibility of their fair countrywomen. The undeniable
notoriety of this circumſtance, added to the penetration and
ſound judgment which otherwiſe always accompany Mr. Zim-
merman's obſervations, would almoſt induce one to ſuppoſe he
had ſome other nation in view in this paſſage ; but the other
parts of it ſeem not ſo applicable to any other.

and

and an unjuſt contempt for our enemies. A nation that thinks itſelf brave, when it does not poſſeſs any bravery, or not in ſuch a ſuperlative degree as it imagines, looks down with conceited vanity on its foes, which no diſappointment, no defeat, no loſs, no unequivocal proof of its weakneſs, can remove.

Tigranes was ſunk in the deepeſt indolence and ſecurity, when Lucullus marched to attack him. It was firmly believed that the Roman general, as ſoon as he came within ſight only of his formidable enemy, would be panic ſtruck, and fly even beyond Aſia. The Romans appeared: Tigranes expreſſed his vexation that all their generals did not come to face him at once; his army amounted to two hundred and ſixty thouſand men, the Roman legions to ſcarcely ten thouſand; a handful of men, too inſignificant and too contemptible to be worth the regard of the numerous hoſt of Armenians. Tigranes obſerved to his courtiers, that they came in too great number for ambaſſadors, and by far too few for enemies: there was not one of his generals, who did not requeſt his leave to go and catch this covey that had imprudently ventured itſelf within the fowler's reach. By break of day, the next morning, when the Armenians were intent on ſurrounding the Romans, they perceived a movement in the camp of Lucullus. Tigranes thought he was about to begin his flight; ſuddenly the

cagles

eagles of the firft legion wheeled to the right, and
the cohorts followed them. Are thefe people coming
againft us ? faid Tigranes, awakened at once from
his long trance. They immediately fell upon the Armenians, and foon, as ordered by Lucullus, they
engaged in clofe fight, which quickly difconcerted
and routed this large hoft, who were only competent
to combat at a diftance : the cavalry fell back on
the infantry, and put it into diforder, and the whole
army was, in a fhort time, completely routed ;
the battle did not laft longer than that of Rofbach,
and this fignal defeat of the Armenians coft the
Romans no more than fix killed, and about one
hundred wounded.

An imaginary valour of another kind, is that of the
Abyffinians. When father Lobo waited on a king
of that country to pay his refpects, juft as he was
about to open his mouth, about twenty fturdy fellows fell upon him and gave him a hearty drub-
bing ; the father flew to the door, where he was
moft refpectfully treated, and was told, that
this beating was an immemorial cuftom, which had
been adopted to fhew to every ftranger, that the
Abyffinians were the moft courageous people of the
earth, and that therefore every other ought to be
humbled before them.

The

The pride arifing from imaginary power, confifts in too high an eftimate of our ftrength. Xerxes, for example, caufed chains to be thrown into the fea in order to fetter it, and had three hundred ftripes inflicted on its turbulent waves for having broken down one of his bridges. He wrote to mount Athos, " Haughty Athos, thou who lifteft up thy head to the fkies, prefume not to oppofe to my labourers rocks through which they cannot penetrate, or I will hew thee down, and hurl thee into the ocean." Oriental pride retains, in our days, the fame character of hyperbolical inflation ; fo that to take their expreffions according to their literal meaning, the Afiatic princes would fupply on earth the place of the Divinity in every point. The king of Malacca ftiles himfelf lord of the winds, and of the eaftern and weftern oceans. The Mogul affumes the title of conqueror of the world, and king of the earth ; and the grandees of his court are no lefs than rulers of the thunder-ftorm, fteerfmen of the whirlwind, or exterminators of hofts.

The petty infignificant tribe of the Natches was, according to their own tradition, the moft powerful nation of the continent of North America; its chief nobility confifted of five hundred Suns, under the control of one great Sun. The prefent fovereign of this little people has a particularity in his pride, which cannot fail to excite much merriment: every

morning

morning he ftalks out of his hovel, bids the fun good morrow, offers him his pipe to fmoke, and points out to him with his finger the courfe which he is to take that day.

In like manner a too exalted opinion entertained of the national confideration conftitutes pride. It has been obferved, that there is hardly a Frenchman who does not attribute to himfelf part of the honour of the Siam embaffy, of which he is particularly vain. The French, in this refpect, often render the national pride which is otherwife juftly founded on the grandeur of their kings, or the conduct and fame of their minifters and generals, ridiculous, by applying to themfelves the perfonal merit of thofe eminent characters. A French colonel, once paffing through Bruffels as a traveller, and having a leifure day, took it into his head to go to the great affembly; he was told, that it was held at the palace of a prince; *tant mieux*, fays he; "What is that to me?"—"But princes only frequent it, fir; and unlefs you are a prince"—" Oh, thefe princes are the moft good-natured people in the world," interrupted the officer; " when the city was taken laft year, I had a dozen of them dancing attendance in my antichamber, and they were all exceffively complaifant."

The

The abbot of Muri in Switzerland is a prince of the holy Roman empire, and he has his four great officers of ſtate; his hereditary marſhals are the noble and illuſtrious the lords of Thurn; his hereditary chamberlains, the lords of Wittenbach; his hereditary cup-bearers, the noble family of the Rupplins; and his hereditary grand carvers, that of Nideroſt : while the ſalary of the chief of theſe officers, the hereditary marſhal, is twenty florins * a year. Strangers are invited to court to dinner, which though ſerved up in great ſtate, is no better than a tradeſman's ordinary. His ſerene highneſs has his own covered body-diſhes ſet before him, which no one of the gueſts is to touch ; he drinks of his own high and illuſtrious body-wine ; while both the ſtrangers and the domeſtics muſt be content with new wine of the laſt vintage.

When the Khan of Tartary, who has not ſo much as a houſe, and who ſubſiſts ſolely on rapine, has finiſhed his repaſt of mare's-milk and horſe-fleſh in his tent, he cauſes an herald to proclaim, that all kings, princes, and potentates of the earth, now have his permiſſion to go to dinner.

But I do not recollect a more glaring inſtance of pride, ariſing from an imaginary conſideration, nor

---

* A florin is 20d.

do

do I think it can well be carried farther, than in a negro king on the coaſt of Guinea, whoſe memory, has been perpetuated by the celebrated author of the Perſian Letters. Some Frenchmen, who landed in his dominion to buy freſh proviſions, were carried before the king, who was adminiſtering the weighty concerns of his realm under a tree ; he ſat on his throne, which was a log of wood, with the fame majeſty and confequence as if it had been the golden feat of the Great Mogul, glittering with jewels ; cloſe to him ſtood his regiment of body guards, confiſting of three or four fellows armed with hedge-ſtakes ; his canopy of ſtate was an umbrella held over his head ; both his majeſty and his royal confort were embelliſhed with the inſigniæ of their regal power, a few copper rings and trinkets, and they ſhone forth above their ſubjects, in the jetty gloſſineſs of their ſkins. This auguſt monarch, underſtanding the native country of his viſitors, aſked with much ſerioufneſs, " Am not I much talked of in France ?"

I could have added numberleſs other inſtances of folly appertaining to the kind of pride I have treated of in this chapter, in which I have not at all pleaſed myſelf ; for it feems to me both too ſhort, and too barren, inſtead of being of a proper length, and full of ſtriking remarks ; but I have juſt thought of the anſwer given by Vitellius to a very critical queſ-

tion

tion of the Emperor Caligula, who was fhamelefs enough, not only publicly to maintain that he was defcended from the gods, but to confirm this idea, he afked Vitellius, "If he had not feen him in bed with the moon?" Vitellius, with downcaft eyes, anfwered, "Moft illuftrious emperor, you gods are only vifible to gods, the feeble fight of mortal man cannot reach you."

CHAPTER THE EIGHTH.

OF PRIDE, RESULTING FROM AN IGNORANCE OF FOREIGN AFFAIRS.

THE utter ignorance of foreign affairs, is a soft cushion from which a nation, reposing in ease and self-complacency, casts an indolent look through the medium of self-conceit on every other; despises what it cannot comprehend, and shews its want of knowledge and judgment as ridiculously as the Paris bookseller, who hearing something of the king of Prussia's attachment to books, asked with an appearance of great astonishment, " What! has the king of Prussia also a library ?"

The Italians, though in our times they know better, were long persuaded that all the inhabitants of the countries beyond the Alps were mere barbarians; since, after the taking of Constantinople by the Turks, the sciences first settled themselves in Italy, and thence spread abroad into other countries. An Italian writer said of the Germans, that their brains did not lie in the head, as was the case with other people, but in their back and shoulders; and their universities might be compared to stables where Minerva kept her mules. Baillet, who quotes

this

this fentence, adds, that it is therefore not to be
wondered at, that the wit and fpirit which we admire in the productions of the modern Italians, as
well as thofe of the ancient Romans and Greeks,
are not to be found in German poetry.   Martinelli,
another Italian author, who fome years ago lived
in London, affirms, that Germany has not, to this
day, produced either a poet or a phyfician.   It is
but a little while ago fince I read in a pamphlet,
publifhed by one Count Roncalli, an Italian phyfician, that inoculation had not been adopted by any
nation of learning.   Did not the right honourable
fcribbler then know, that the practice is become
general throughout Europe, and that, in our enlightened times, every European nation that is in
its right fenfes, takes for itfelf the lead in literature, and that all unanimoufly affign to the Englifh
the fecond place, among whom inoculation is univerfally practifed?

The Germans have by moft people been abufed,
as the beafts of burden of the literary world, the
cinder-fifters and hod-men, raking together and
preparing the mortar and materials for the edifice
of letters.   I read a few years ago, in one of the
beft Englifh reviews, that the German writers have,
from time immemorial poffeffed the fame privilege with theologifts, that of writing many books,
and faying little in them ; that they are famous for
fcraping together matter wherewith to fill many
unwieldy

unwieldy folios, fpinning out their works to a formidable length, and wearying the patience of their
reader without informing his underftanding; and
finally, that every German head contained a con-
fufed medley of books, ever in a litter, and the
more looked into the lefs underftood. Full as injurious would it be in me to call all the Englifh
• barbarians, only becaufe, even in thefe days of
knowledge, at the public difputations at Oxford on
Afh-Wednefday, a young Englifh pedant, dreft out
like a mafquerader at Shrove-tide, mounts the rof-
trum, and lifts the impenetrable fhield of Ariftotelian
quirks and quibbles, againft the leaden darts which
his opponents, reprefenting the fons of Scotus,
Burgerdicius, and Smiglefius, aim at the doughty
champion.

A minifter of ftate in Perfia knows as much of
European affairs, as he does of what is tranfacted
in the moon. Moft of the Perfians think our part
of the world is a fmall ifland in the northern waters,
which produces nothing that is good or beautiful;
for why elfe, fay they, do the Europeans fetch fuch
things from us, if they were to be got in their own
country?

The Chinefe underftand by the four quarters of
the globe little more than their empire; they have
the moft unbounded contempt for all other countries, and they entertain a notion that all the heavenly

venly bodies watch over China alone, without any kind of concern for any other land. They take the earth to be a vaſt horizontal ſquare; and they look upon China, which they ſay lies in the middle, as occupying not only the beſt, but the largeſt portion of it. Accordingly they ſtile their country Chong-que, or the kingdom of the middle, and Tien-Hia, or all under the heavens. A jeſuit miſ-ſionary, to flatter theſe opinions, in a map of the world which he made for the Chineſe, placed China in the middle, an artifice well worthy of the inven-tion of a jeſuit. As to their own maps, in them the Chineſe give their empire the greateſt extent on earth, and ſcatter the reſt of the world in the form of very ſmall iſlands, here and there all round China. Their geographers give theſe iſlands or king-doms the moſt ludicrous names, and tell the moſt ridiculous ſtories about them ; one they call Seao-ginque, or the region of the dwarfs, of whom they relate, that they are obliged to live as cloſely toge-ther as bees in a hive, for fear of being ſnatched away by the eagles and vultures ; another is Chuen-finque, or the kingdom whoſe inhabitants have a large hole in their breaſts, into which they put a ſtick, and carry one another about on their backs ; and a pack of the like nonſenſe. However, ſince the Chineſe, by their communication with us, know a little more of Europe, they have advanced it in their maps to the ſize of one of the Canary iſlands.

All

All other nations muſt eſteem it a very great honour, if they are admitted to be accounted the ſubjeĉts of China; they are, themſelves, exceedingly ſhy of ſending any ambaſſadors abroad, becauſe they look upon an embaſſy, a preſent, or even a letter from any foreign country, as a moſt poſitive proof of reſpeĉtful ſubmiſſion, and an acknowledgment of the right of China to exaĉt tribute of that nation; accordingly its name is immediately inſcribed in a regiſter kept for the purpoſe, and appears in the annals of China as a tributary kingdom, the number whereof is very conſiderable; as every man who brings a letter to China from any prince or ſtate, is called an ambaſſador, and his ſovereign a ſlave of China.

The emperor Yong-Tching ſaid in a ſpeech to the jeſuits: " I am the abſolute lord of the kingdom of the middle; all other ſtates, great and ſmall, ſend me tribute; it amuſes me ſometimes to inſtruĉt them; if they receive and attend to my leſſons, well and good, if not, I turn them adrift." It was in 1758 that the jeſuits tried to bring the miniſters of the Chineſe empire to admit of an embaſſy from France, but they were refuſed it, as they had ſecretly given them to underſtand, " that his moſt chriſtian majeſty was not tributary to the emperor of China; that the preſents, which the emperor might ſend to the king of France, would not be looked on as proceeding ſolely from the bounty of

9

the

the imperial donor, and that the king's letters were not to be accounted petitions, nor the emperor's anfwers, commands."

The Japanefe are fools of the fame ftamp. Niphon, the name which they commonly give to their country, imports light of the fun, becaufe, being unacquainted with any lands to the eaftward, they fuppofe the fun rifes to them the firft; they are ignorant of the fpheric form of the earth, and that every country lies eaft and weft with refpect to them. Another name of Japan, which occurs in their books, is Tenka; but this feems to be not fo much a proper name, as a figurative appellation, which is adopted by the Japanefe out of vanity: it means, the region that is under the heavens; whence, likewife, comes the title that is alfo given to the emperor of Japan, of Tenka-fama, or the monarch under the heavens; which is very applicable to the idea formerly entertained by this people, that theirs was the only inhabited country, themfelves the only human beings, and all other lands the refidence of devils and unclean fpirits.

We thus fee, that the lefs any nation is acquainted with foreign affairs, the more it exalts itfelf; and its vanity finds its account in this ignorance, on which it grounds the moft foolifh contempt for all other countries.

CHAPTER THE NINTH.

OF PRIDE AS ARISING FROM IGNORANCE IN GENERAL.

As ignorance and a want of felf-knowledge engender felf-complacency and an unjuft contempt for others; fo the pride that refults from general ignorance in a nation, is the fame with too high an eftimation of its own knowledge, however contracted and defective this may be.

The French have been accufed, that they think their laws are fo excellent, that they ought to be followed by every other nation; they would not be fo vain of their laws, if the multitude knew that there is fcarcely any knowledge of the law of nature or of nations to be met with in France, where we fhould the moft expect to meet with it; that in the numerous fchools and univerfities with which that kingdom abounds, where fo many things of no real worth are taught with the greateft affiduity and pedantry, there is not one profefforfhip for the law of nations; and that of courfe the French are the only nation who feem to believe that this fcience is of no utility.

They

They would not, I fay, be fo vain of their laws, if the opinion of one of their own great men was more commonly known among them; who main-tains that their whole legiflature, formed out of the confufion of the feudal fyftem, is a monftrous and unwieldy ftructure, which refembles a moft incon-fiftent heap of ruins; that the law, which ought to be the exact counterpart of univerfal order, is on the contrary exceedingly contradictory to it, and inftead of uniting its fubjects, divides them; making as it were, a hundred different ftates in the bofom of one kingdom.

The haughty Englifh are equally blind in this refpect, thefe felf-fufficient Iflanders look on their common law, which is the fole and beft guide fol-lowed in the royal courts of juftice, as the only rule of right, and fuch a wonder of perfection, that Chancellor Fortefcue, in the work he publifhed in 1469 in praife thereof, holds it almoft a fin to doubt its all-fufficiency; neverthelefs, this rule of law is faid to be founded, for the moft part, on maxims adopted long ago, and the confequences deducible from them have all a legal authority, although they are not unfrequently contradictory and inconfiftent; and what is more, although England maintains a ftanding army of upwards of forty thoufand lawyers, yet it may confidently be afferted, that there is no country on earth, where a more deplorable ignorance

of

of their own laws prevails than there. Near three centuries ago, it required twenty years ftudy to acquire
a due knowledge of the laws of England ; and yet,
by the villanous manœuvres of the unworthy profeffors of the law, the numerous propofals made for
reformation of the common law, and the commif-
fioners feveral times appointed by parliament for
the purpofe of improving the fyftem of jurifpru-
dence, have all been fruftrated and rendered of no
avail : nay in 1659*, the lawyers obtained a promife, in return for a contribution of one hundred
thoufand pounds fterling, that they fhould remain
in the undifturbed poffeffion of all the juridical
abufes ; and in the fame year, William Cole wrote
a treatife, to prove that the lawyers in England
were the greateft rogues and cheats in the kingdom.

Spain produces in its hot and parched climate
fome very keen and penetrating geniufes ; but the

* This was one of the leaft iniquitous modes of extorting
money, adopted in 1659 by the rump parliament (fo called in
derifion, as being compofed of the bafeft and moft contemptible
members of the long parliament) during the protectorate of
Richard Cromwell; and as this affembly was never confidered a
legal one, it is unfair therefore to adduce this as an inftance of
folly in our government; and certainly more irrelevant to conclude from it, that our laws have ever fince remained in exactly
the fame ftate ; for very material alterations have been made in
them fince that period, and hardly a feffion of parliament paffes
without refcinding from or adding to them.

ever

ever predominating love of the marvellous, which . is fo remarkable in this nation, diftorts and fpoils - nature, the only model for all that is fublime and beautiful. The fciences remain always in Spain, for very obvious reafons, in a very wretched fituation; yet they entertain fuch lofty ideas of their own fuperiority in this refpeʼct, that it long was a prevalent opinion among the Spaniards, that God converfed with Mofes on Mount Sinai in the Spanifh language, and revealed to them long ago all the many fecrets and hidden myfteries of nature, which yet are the objeʼcts of the diligent refearches and inquiries among the moft learned philofophers of the world. Conformably to this tradition, they give fome of their colleges of learning the moft inflated appellations : one is called the Olympian, and another the Radient College, or Academy.

The judgment of a whole nation muft not be arraigned on account of the enthufiaftic exclamations of fome hot-headed divines. Yet the innumerable panegyrics, which, from the introduʼction to Torrubia's Natural Hiftory of Spain, publifhed in 1754, have fomething in them very aptly characteriftic of the national charaʼcter of the Spaniards, although I very readily make allowance for fome exceptions : one of thefe encomiafts, father Hieronimus of Salamanca, exclaims : " Even if I had a hundred tongues, and if each of them, nay if every
individual

individual part of my body, every joint, every vein, was endowed with the faculty of the moſt eloquent language ; yet how very unfit, how totally unable ſhould I be to exprefs the delight which the peruſal of this Natural Hiſtory afforded me." In the confidence that all Europe pays the moſt profound attention to him, the reverend father goes on; "Behold, ſays he, Torrubia, the crowned lion of Spain, the modern Geryon, a philoſopher who has ſurpriſed nature in the fact, a wonder of literature, to whom nothing riſes ſuperior, ſave his own immortal Natural Hiſtory. He is the favoured child of providence, who beſtowed every advantage on him, adding as an enhancement to them all, the ineſtimable bleſſing of being born in Spain. Happy favoured Spain ! thou faithful genius of our nation, thou art ever conſtant, ever enlightened, ever invincible, ever . triumphant over ignorance and error !"

The Chineſe are highly celebrated for learning, and it is ſaid they are exceedingly vain of it ; but as it appears to me, it is of their ignorance that they are vain ; the moſt extravagant notions are formed of China, as the travellers who have given us an account of it are often very partial to the wonderful, yet their relations, at the ſame time, carry very much an air of probability. Look on the large and magnificent libraries of China, the aſtoniſhing number of their colleges, of their graduates, of their

H   obſerv-

obfervatories, the extreme attention which they pay
to the contemplation of the heavens; confider, that
learning is the only road to honour and dignity;
that talents and knowledge form the only rule of
preferment; that by the fundamental laws of the
empire, which have been moſt ſtrictly obſerved for
a long ſeries of centuries, none but a man of learning can ever attain to the dignity of governor of a
city or a province; and that all the courts of juſtice
muſt likewiſe be filled with perfons of literary abilities; add to this, that the cuſtoms and manners of
the Chineſe have remained invariable, amidſt the
greateſt revolutions; that their conquerors even have
adopted them; that the reign of the law has never
been ſuſpended or weakened; that their empire has
feen the downfal of every other; and that amidſt
the ruins of the world, their's only has remained
erect and unſhaken; and you will certainly be induced to believe that the Chineſe excel all other
nations in every kind of human knowledge; yet
try it by the touchſtone of candid and ſerious examination, and the enchantment will vaniſh, and the
nation ſo much extolled above others will ſink below the general level, and appear in a very mortifying point of view.

The Chineſe ſtudy their own language moſt at-
tentively, and well they may, for to underſtand it
perfectly, it would employ the greateſt part of their

            lives.

lives. After they have attained a knowledge of the grammar, they apply themfelves to Hiftory, Law, and Morality. Whoever wifhes to be created doctor, and who thus ftrives to attain one of the chief dignities of the empire, muft be thoroughly acquainted with the language; he muft be able to write, which is by no means an eafy matter; he muft be able to prepare a difcourfe in the beft ftyle, on morality, or on the art of government; and in the Chinefe academies, a chief part of education confifts in the art of making a genteel bow, of giving or receiving a cup of tea with a fuitable grace, how to walk, and how to carry a parafol with a becoming air. One of their books of inftruction, on thefe important points alone, contains three thoufand rules.

This is all very well, fay the champions for Chinefe fuperiority; yet it is only by poffeffing a thorough knowledge of their language that they can become acquainted with their own laws and cuftoms, with the actions of their forefathers, and the hiftory of their empire; but they do not attend to the circumftance, that many a Chinefe ftudent dies of old age before he has learned to read. Their nonfenfical pedantry, with refpect to external appearances, is held by fome to be very important and praife-worthy; the reverence they fhew, by bowing to the ground, or kneeling before each other, on faying good morrow or good night, is admired and interpreted as a proof

of

of the esteem they have both for themselves and others. It is alleged, that this knowledge of the exact measure of respect due to every rank and every ramification of rank, acts as a great restraint on personal pride; that it preserves a due distinction between the different orders, and prevents equality among mankind; that it bows the neck of the man who is but a hair's breadth lower in rank, in obedience to his superior. But these arguments are only worthy of such as are born and educated slaves, and certainly ought not to be adduced in honour of the Chinese; for mutual esteem exists in the heart, and not in a graceful bow or an unmeaning compliment.

The Chinese are in reality unfit for the more useful arts and sciences, notwithstanding they appear proficients in them; they know a little of every thing, but nothing in perfection. Almost all the arts have been known and practised in China for time immemorial, but they remain in the same state as they were at their commencement; and of some they are wholly ignorant.

Their constitution and government have been extolled above all others in the world; yet the people are every where the prey to rogues of quality, and are often in danger of starving, by the iniquitous administration of their protectors and parents, as the

governors

governors there are indifcriminately ftyled. Very
good laws, it is true, are enacted in China, as well
as in other countries, but they are not obferved;
for the great panacea, gold, makes amends for the
worft infractions of them. To be fure, the Chinefe
government fo far refembles the patriarchal authority, to which they pretend it is finally reducible, that
their mandarins, like loving fathers, beftow many
fevere drubbings upon their children, whom, as to
any other proofs of paternal love and care, they
very generoufly leave to pine away in mifery, for
fear the population of the empire fhould become too
great. Politics are fo little known and underftood
there, that the Chinefe have no conception of any
other government than a defpotic monarchy, and
they can never be brought to comprehend the poffi-
bility of the exiftence of a republic; and their civil
laws are often diametrically oppofite to the natural
and moft important duties of life. In fhort, let their
patriarchal form of government, which has been fo
much cried up, appear ever fo mild and favourable
to its fubjects in theory or in practice, it is certain
that there is no nation on earth more plundered, oppreffed, and robbed by the great, than the Chinefe.

Their fyftem of morality has been exalted to the
fkies; yet it evidently aims at fubjecting even the
hearts of the people to the will of a defpot, and
therefore publicly makes morality fubfervient to
policy. This error of the Chinefe legiflator has

rendered

rendered manly virtue an object of indifference to the people, while the care taken to enforce obedience and fubmiffion to one head, has likewife introduced a fpirit of hypocrify and diffimulation, very inconfiftent with good morals. Thefe inculcate and produce an artlefs fincerity, and an undeceiving candour, in both of which the Chinefe are remarkably deficient ; for there is no nation upon the face of the earth more given to low cunning and every kind of fraud ; they are certainly moft oftentatioufly virtuous : the women do not only fhun the company of men, on every vifible occafion, but the greateft care is taken that they fhould not come together, even in the invifible world ; for the body of a female is carefully depofited at a proper diftance from that of a male in their burial places ; but who is ignorant, that the more fhew is made of virtue and chaftity, the more fcope is left for fufpicion, and that where appearances pafs current for honour and honefty, little of the realities is to be found ?

Nor, finally, am I furprifed, that the Chinefe indulge in the moft wanton exceffes; that they thruft their children out of doors, without remorfe ; that they bribe their midwives to drown their girls as foon as born in a tub of water, when they fuppofe their maintenance would be too expenfive; for how can they believe, in earneft, in the excellence of virtue, when almoft all their learned

men

men deny the immortality of the foul; maintain that matter and nature are immeafurable,
infinite, and uncreated; that their operations and
motions are uninterrupted, irrefiftible, and without
beginning or end; and deduce from the continu-
ance of their agency, the production both of fouls
and bodies, the duration of whofe exiftence again,
they fuppofe, is in proportion to the part every being can feize of the univerfal fubftance; who, in
fact, are downright atheifts?

They do not meddle much with natural philofophy, nor are they able to form a proper conception
of any one operation of nature. Their aftronomy
is very ancient, they are faid to have ftudied hard at
it for four thoufand years, and yet, before the arrival of the jefuits, they could not make a correct
almanac. The court of mathematicians, confift-
ing of a prefident, two affeffors, and many fubordinate mandarins, fuperintends all matters of aftronomy, and publifhes the imperial calendar, by which
the people are acquainted what days and what hours
are lucky or unlucky. Their moft important bufinefs is to predict eclipfes, the calculations of which
they prefent to the emperor, who fends them to the
court of cuftoms, whence they are diftributed
through all the provinces of the empire, that
the appropriate ceremonies, appointed in fuch
cafes, may every where be duly obferved. Thefe

ceremonies

ceremonies are of great confequence ; for they confift chiefly in beating of drums continually during the
eclipfe, while the people raife their voices in howlings and lamentations, in order, by this diabolical
noife, to drive away the dragon, who is fuppofed to
be about to devour the fun or the moon.

In medicine, it is pretended, the Chinefe can perform wonders; they are, perhaps, as good as our
quacks, and indeed, not inferior to fuch of our
European doctors, who attempt to perfuade the
public, they can put difeafe and death to flight
with a fingle pill ; but they are entirely ignorant of
anatomy, and have the moft wretched ideas refpecting the properties and utility of the feveral parts of
the body; they of courfe know nothing of the
proximate caufes of diftempers, the knowledge of
which, is the only true foundation to proceed upon
in the cure of them. They are fuppofed to poffefs
the moft extraordinary knowledge of that part of
medicine, relating to the pulfe; like our water-doc-
tors and palmifters, they fecretly make the moft
exact enquiries refpecting the fituation and circumftances of the patient, before they venture to pronounce with certainty, what fuch or fuch a kind of
pulfation denotes ; and if the evils they have pre-
dicted do not come to pafs, they know how to help
the patient to them, for the honour of their knowledge in the art of prognoftication. The maxims of
this

this art are very limited, regular, and fyftematic; if the pulfe beats hard, the kidneys muft be inflamed; if it is fomething like the pecking of a bird, the patient muft die the next morning between ten and eleven o'clock; in fact, the whole of the art of medicine in China confifts in this knack of lying with a good grace, from the ftate of the pulfe, and in the knowledge of fome fimples which defcend from father to fon, and in the hands of fuch fools, naturally become, without exception, fpecifics for almoft all diforders.

Of their art of war, fome judgment may be formed from the circumftance that there is always a gownfman, that is to fay, a man of letters, who accompanies their armies, and to whom all their generals are fubordinate. On a march, the man in the long robe is placed in the front, but when a battle is fought, he takes his ftand fome miles in the rear; provided only, that he may be near enough to communicate his orders to the army under his control, and at the fame time fo fituated, as to lead the van of the run-aways, if his party be defeated.

The Chinefe are praifed for their inventive genius in the arts; and yet no Chinefe artift can make a fingle firelock; for it is but a few years ago that they made ufe of match-locks, and did not know

what

what flints were. They have not yet been able to learn how to repair a watch when it is out of order; it is dead, they fay, and barter it away for a living one. They imagine they have invented mufic, and have even brought it to perfection; what they have, is too bad to be called mufic, it is even faid to be worfe than the French*. As to their painting, it poffeffes no excellence but a brilliancy of colouring, and is otherwife formal, fpiritlefs, and abfurd; they caricature their own faces, and put themfelves in the moft grotefque poftures, although they in fact look pretty well, except their bellies, which are too pro‑minent. They have an utter diflike to European manners, dreffes, and cuftoms; and are fo far averfe to our architecture, that it was with the greateft difficulty the Chinefe builders could be brought to erect the church, that the jefuits formerly had in the emperor's palace at Pekin, according to the model fent from Europe. Although they cannot but look with aftonifhment at the fize and ftructure of our fhips, they think themfelves affronted as well as fcoffed at, when they are invited to imitate them. Their poetry is exceffively phlegmatic and infipid, without any flights to pleafe the imagination, or in‑tereft to affect the paffions. They are, moreover, faid to have invented the theatre; but in the Thef‑pian art too, they have not got beyond the very

* The French tranflator has a note here: "On voit bien que c'eft un *Allemand* qui parle," *We fee plainly it is a* German *who fpeaks.*

firft

firft rudiments. And with all this ignorance, their contempt for other nations is fo decided, that they will not adopt the moft fimple, and evidently the moft ufeful inventions of the Europeans; nay, they are fo averfe even to their affiftance, that at a fire in Canton, they chofe rather to fuffer the greateft part of the town to be burnt, than permit the Englifh failors of Commodore Anfon's fhip to extinguifh the flames, which they were not able to do themfelves, and were forely offended at the alacrity of the tars on that occafion, becaufe there was no formal per- miffion given by the viceroy to ftop the confla- gration.

But the Chinefe, it is pretended, underftood all the neceffary arts, and fuch as are of real utility, upwards of four thoufand years ago; and notwith- ftanding we now boaft fo much of the progrefs we have made in thofe arts, we at that period could neither read nor write. It has, however, been omitted to be mentioned, what particular arts of fuch effential ufefulnefs could flourifh among the Chinefe, when they were even unpractifed in the primary fimple occupations of hunting and fifh- ing; when they could hardly provide themfelves food; when they had neither clothes nor dwellings; for all thefe arts were not only totally unknown to them, according to their own acknowledgment, in the pretended reign of the emperor Fo-Hi, but they

were

were mere favages near a thoufand years afterwards, when the Egyptians taught them to write, and gave them laws and cuftoms.   To this again is replied, difpute as long as you pleafe about the fourteen emperors who reigned before Fo-Hi, all you may fay will end in the acknowledgment, that China was then very populous, and was governed by a regular code of laws.   Now the annals of thefe very times, declared to be wholly fabulous by the viceroy Nien-Hy-Iao, fay, that mankind then lived like brutes, wandering through the forefts ; that the women were in common; that no other thought was entertained then, except for prefent fubfiftence; that animals were eat with fkin, hair, and all, and birds with their feathers, and their blood ferved for drink ; that raw hides were the only clothing ; and in fhort, that Fo-Hi firft taught them both hunting and fifhing.   Yet, neverthelefs, it is maintained, that the Chinefe could write before they knew how to make bread, and that the hiftory of thefe bril-liant ages have been tranfmitted to us by the literati of thofe remote and favage times.

What, however, renders the Chinefe moft con-temptible is, the prevalence of fuperftition amongft them, which ufurps the place of religion in every breaft.   The memory of the reign of Tching-Tfong, the third emperor of the nineteenth dynafty, has in particular been ftigmatized by

the

the favour fhewn under his government to every
fpecies of bigotry, and the encouragement of religious juggling. And though, as we have before
mentioned, they are in general atheifts, they are not
the only people amongft whom fuperftition is found
coupled with atheifm.

Evil fpirits are in their opinion agents in the moft
common occurrences. They have a kind of ballot
or lottery, by which they difcover whether they
may begin a journey, whether they may buy or fell,
whether they may marry their children fortunately
or unfortunately; they take the greateft pains to
find out by their arts of divination the moft advantageous fpot on which to erect a houfe, the quarter
towards which they muft make the opening of the
door; the day moft propitious for the building of a
kiln; which hill or eminence to chufe for the moft
comfortable burying-place; and this laft point is of
fuch great confequence, that when a man excels in
wit or learning, the merit is not his own, a fudden
elevation to any honour or dignity is not attributed
to defert, or fuccefs in trade, to induftry or penetration, but all is afcribed to the proper choice of a
place of burial for his forefathers.

The power of impoftors over weak minds is no
where fo great as in China; no where are fortune-
tellers

tellers and aftrologers held in fuch eftimation as there; the markets and ftreets fwarm with people of this defcription, who make open profeffion of their bufinefs, and hang out a fign like other tradef-men; nothing is ever done in China without firft confulting thefe conjurers, whofe lying prognoftica-tions are imprinted with the ftamp of eternal truth in the eyes of their admirers.   A Chinefe, who may have been perfuaded by one of thefe magicians, that he is unable to beget children, will every time his wife is pregnant of a child, of his own procreation, think her an adultrefs; he will rather embitter the life of an honeft woman, and fill his head with the moft tormenting ideas of imaginary cuckoldom, than avoid by kindnefs the giving occafion to his wife to ferve him in reality the trick he has been made to fufpect.

The almanac which is publifhed every year, under the infpection and with the approbation of the emperor, and of the court of mathematicians, contains, befides a few aftronomical calculations, a fpecification of what days and hours are lucky or unlucky; the days on which phlebotomy is advife-able, the minute moft aufpicious to beg any favour of the emperor, the hours when to pay honours to the deceafed, when to make offerings, when to mar-ry, when to build, when to invite friends, and in general,

general, when to attend to almoſt every public and private occupation; this almanac is in the hands of every body, and is the ſummary of all the knowledge of many families, and an oracle for all China.

In addition to theſe egregious faults, and to this deplorable ignorance, there is no nation on earth more addicted to pride and arrogance than the Chineſe. In their opinion, they excel all mankind in ability and knowledge, which they poſſeſs in as great a degree as human nature is capable of ; and, prepoſſeſſed in the extreme in favour of their manners and principles, they cannot conceive that any thing they do not practiſe can be right, nor any thing their learned men are ignorant of, can be true.

And thus the moſt defective knowledge is a ſource of pride, to a nation which perceives nothing wanting in itſelf, nor any thing good in others ; which thinks itſelf only enlightened and wiſe, and all others both blind and ſtupid.

CHAPTER THE TENTH.

REFLECTIONS ON THE BENEFITS AND EVILS OF NATI-
ONAL PRIDE FOUNDED UPON IMAGINARY
ADVANTAGES.

Round Cape Horn, and fo through Terra Auf-
tralis Incognita to the Devil, is the journey every
philofopher wifhes to the prejudices of all other
men, while he remains firmly attached to his own;
yet prejudices muft, and ought fo far to exift among
mankind as they are ufeful.

There is certainly a degree of national pride
arifing only from prejudice, that is of great political utility. Self-conceit is productive of hope and
fear in a nation; the latter preferves men from the
commiffion of crimes, the former invites them to
the care of felf-intereft and to diligence. From felf-
conceit proceeds likewife vanity, and from this laft,
the defire of rifing above one's ftation; the love of
oftentation, emulation, arts, fafhions, good manners,
and tafte; vanity and pride are therefore in the
hands of found policy very ufeful follies, for they
are born with us, die with us, never tire, and have
often the appearance of virtues.

I   The

The love of our country is little more in many cafes, than the love of an afs for his manger. But the intelligent and accomplifhed Lady Mary Wortley Montague, after a long courfe of travels through Afia, Africa, and the greateft part of Europe, was firmly of opinion that an honeft Englifh country gentleman was the happieft of men; for he does not trouble his head to know, nor indeed would he believe, that Greek wine is better than ftout ale; he is convinced that the richeft fruits of Africa have neither the fine yellow tints nor the fine flavour of his golden pippin; that Italian *becafico* are nothing like fo nice as a piece of roaft beef; in fhort, that there can be no perfect enjoyment out of Old England.

We always muft contemplate with pleafure a nation which loves itfelf, exalts its own countrymen, prefers its own manufactures to thofe of foreigners, efteems its own writers, and by having the higheft opinion of itfelf, and all that belongs to it, is as happy as poffible, either in imagination or reality, for both are the fame. Let, therefore, our philofophy call the prejudices which arife from education ever fo deftructive and miftaken, which make a Moor believe his country the fineft in the world, and that God himfelf was at the trouble of creating Ethiopia, while the other parts of the globe were made by his deputed angels;

or

or thofe which induce a Laplander to feek for an earthly paradife among his Norwegian and pri-mæval fnows, or a Swifs, as the penetrating Doctor Smollet fays in his Travels, to prefer the barren mountain of Soleure to the fertile plains of Lombardy; fuffer others to behold their own country with partiality; fuffer them, like the peafants round San Marino, to believe that they are the only good and honeft men on earth; fuffer them to take the little circle that forms their horizon for the rule of all poffible exten-fion, and let their governors be wifely anxious to give the greateft importance and extent to the trifling interefts of the fmall tract, beyond which they think there is nothing worthy of a thought, at leaft, let the fpace be ever fo un-bounded on the other fide of the hedge, they care not about it, but think there is a Deity who will at-tend to the whole; for content makes happy fathers, happy citizens, and happy fubjects, with no better fare than black bread, hard cheefe, and butter-milk.

This is all I can fay in favour of that fpecies of national pride, founded on imaginary advantages. It would be a good excufe for this pride, and an alle-viation of the ill it caufes, in confequence of its at-tendant contempt, if it could with any juftice be faid that contempt leffens hatred as much as it does

envy,

envy, which is the painful and corroding forrow pervading the mind on the perception of another's happinefs or good fortune. Whoever envies a rich man for his wealth, finds his envy leffened, when he plainly perceives that this Crœfus is a fool; who-ever envies a man of learning for his fcience, is fure to find his envy diminifh, if he can perfuade himfelf, that his worldly knowledge rifes infinitely fuperior to that of this man of letters. But hatred confifts in wifhing for the calamity of another: an enemy, for inftance, is a fubject of hatred in proportion as he awakens our fears; he may be inexpreffibly contemptible, but his power may be great; and we fhall never ceafe hating him till his power can have no influence either on our happinefs or mifery.

The mutual hatred of nations for each other, however, in nowife decreafes by their mutual con-tempt; the Greeks were full as much animated by both paffions againft the Perfians; the populace among Chriftians look on the Jews, without ex-ception, as dead to every fentiment of virtue and benevolence, and deeply funk in the moft con-temptible covetoufnefs, ufury, and villany. It is, therefore, almoft an article of religion, and a meri-torious work, to perfecute the Jews on account of the abhorrence which is felt for them; and to hate them becaufe they are contemned and defpifed. Con-

tempt

tempt and hatred for another nation, are no where united with more force and expreffion than in the Englifh againft the French. A foreigner, if not dreffed like an Englifhman, is in great danger of being affailed with dirt for being thought a French-man; but in a thoufand inftances the French re-turn this contempt. We may form, without ex-ception, very juft conclufions of their other opinions refpecting the Englifh, from the French accounts of the warlike actions of their valiant neighbours; of which the Jumonville of M. Thomas is a remark-able inftance. This is an heroic poem, in which the national hate and luft of revenge has infpired the author, one of the greateft geniufes and moft up-right men of France, to take occafion, from the firing of three or four guns from a fmall fort and the death of about eight Frenchmen, to fet up a lamentation as if it was a St. Bartholomew's maffacre. The French hate the Spaniards in the fame manner, becaufe they defpife them. In the campaign in Italy of 1746, the greateft exafperation broke out on numberlefs occafions between thofe nations, who were then allies, to the great detriment of the operations of war. At Hofpitella, in the middle of the day, a Spanifh regi-ment of cavalry attacked one of the French regi-ments, becaufe they could not agree about their encampment, which was feparated from one another by a high road.

But

But the hate of a nation for foreigners is very often to its extreme detriment univerfal. In England, they acknowledge that the unnatural antipathy of the Englifh for all foreigners, is one of the greateft and moft illiberal caufes which prevents the fettlement and population of the immenfe poffeffions of this nation in America, by the want whereof the growth of trade and profperity is greatly impeded.

Much worfe confequences flow from the contempt which arifes from religious pride. Whoever imagines that no man can be truly eftimable or virtuous, whofe belief does not precifely agree with his own, whoever condemns and renounces thofe who do not think exactly as he does on every point of theology, becomes of courfe an enemy to the greateft part of mankind. The unavoidable confequence of a prepoffeffion of the infallibility of one's church is intoleration; and this again produces a fwarm of venomous prejudices and opinions, which, like the mufquitos in hot countries, are continually peftering us by myriads on all fides, and cannot fail of ftinging thofe who are not armed with the fly-flap of reafon, or the imperforable veil of philofophy.

As long as the hope and expectation is entertained that the whole world will finally adhere

to

to one confeffion of faith, the furtherance of the
grand work of converfion is fuppofed to be the indifpenfable and bounden duty of every individual :
thofe who are thought to wander in darknefs and
error, are therefore not eafily fuffered to live in peace
and quiet. The man, who imagines he is furrounded
by men doomed to eternal damnation, is therefore
a faint, and ever ready to fight the devil in his
own domain ; and the Gofpel of the God of Peace
and Love has therefore been continually debafed and
contaminated by perfecuting and blood-thirfty priefts,
with their appropriate inftruments, fwords and bayo-
nets, gibbets, ftakes, racks, wheels, and chains*.

Thefe opinions have at all times inflamed the
minds of men ; zealous churchmen have ever been
the firft promoters of herefies, and have augmented
the number of heretics, exactly in proportion to
the blindnefs of their zeal and their induftry in difcovering them. Let us take a retrofpect of the
time of the crufades; thefe coft Europe two millions
of fighting men, monks and priefts, with the mafs-
book in one hand and the bloody banner of war in
the other, led the van ; numerous armies of holy
robbers followed them, decorated and confecrated
to the fervice of the Lord by a white crofs ; they
quitted their lawful occupations and refpectable
fituations in the Weft, to become thieves and mur-

* This paffage the French tranflator has thought fit to omit.

derers

derers in the Eaſt; they ſold their poſſeſſions in order to go forth, under the bleſſing of the Lamb of God, to plunder thoſe of the infidels; they abandoned their wives, to deflower virgins and violate matrons, in honour of the Almighty; and, in the reſult, they ſacrificed every conſideration for the benefit of being cut to pieces, in a diſtant but an holy region; and ſent to their long home, polluted with the blood of the innocent, and loaded with the execrations of the inoffenſive inhabitants of the country they had made the ſcene of devaſtation and bloodſhed: and yet their religion, the cauſe for which they fought, was directly oppoſite to the tenets of the Alkoran, againſt which theſe ſanguinary and ruinous expeditions were ſet on foot. The commands of their God were founded on peace, on meekneſs, and on charity; thoſe which Mahomet impoſed on his followers as the will of the Omnipotent, taught that the ſacrifice of themſelves and their property in war, for the conqueſt and conſtraint of infidels, and the eſtabliſhment and enlargement of the true religion, was the greateſt merit; that thoſe who die in battle for the ſake of their faith, live hereafter in immortal happineſs; that the blood ſhed in the cauſe of religion, if but a ſingle drop, is pleaſing to the Deity; and that to watch one night for the defence of the frontiers of the faithful, is more agreeable to Heaven than a rigid faſt of two months.

The

The haughtinefs of religious pride will not ad-·
mit of any toleration ;. it irritates the minds of men
by always attempting to force them to think as we
do ; and this ambition of domineering over the confciences of mankind ·is the true fource of religious
zeal. It has been obferved, that, in common difputes, perverfenefs and obftinacy never reach that
height which they do in the moft trifling religious
controverfies, for in other things almoft every one
is aware that he may be deceived; but, on the contrary, we are always intimately perfuaded of the
·truth of our fyftem of faith, and·are therefore very
angry at thofe of another perfuafion, who, inftead of
conforming to our opinions, are intent upon con-
ftraining us to alter them in compliance with their
own. The pride of religion, and the fpirit of perfecution accompanying it, likewife produces, among
the profeffors of the fame belief, that cruel and fufpicious fpirit of dogmatifm, that inquifitorial auf-
terity which would preclude all neceffity of thought,
and require the moft implicit conformity, in whatever regards their fyftem of theology, and which
would banifh truth and knowledge, together with
the liberty of difquifition from even our Proteftant
religion, if the bitternefs of our zealous controver-
fial writers was not fometimes curbed and kept
under by a biting and fevere farcafm on their untimely and unqualified afperity.

Religious

Religious pride would have its own creed give the law to the belief of all men.   It afcribes to the Supreme Being its own ravings and unreafonable opinion, and makes the maintenance of its theory appertain to the honour of the Godhead. If its principles or its voice fail, arrogance, envy, rancour, and an univerfal hatred for mankind, put on the mafk of religion, and, execute in the name of Lord the moft diabolical revenge : hence came the prefumption, the warmth and violence which were manifeft in the fectaries of the Greek church, who thought themfelves polluted by fpeaking to one of another communion, or by only abiding under the fame roof ; hence came the opinion among the fubjects of the Byzantian emperors, that thofe princes who, in their eyes, were rebellious to their God, could not have been appointed their rulers by Providence, and were therefore not the anointed of the Lord ; hence came the tyrannic fway and inflexible cruelty which fo many fervants of the God of Peace have extolled and enjoined in the worldly judges, whofe aid they have called in to terminate their religious differences ; and hence, even very recently, principles the moft inimical to mankind have fhone forth, with the full fplendour of ftupidity, which characterized the fifteenth and fixteenth centuries, in the Paftoral Letters of the Apoftle of Cracow.

Ever

Ever fince the mild and invifible kingdom of another world has been changed into the moft violent, as well as tangible and apparent defpotifm in this, Chriftianity, violated by the hands of its priefts, has made men hard, auftere, unmerciful; and outrageous; it has put fire and fword into their hands; it has led kings and princes to make a hell of this world, to murder and torture, in the name of the God of Mercy, the fubjects they were bound to cherifh and protect. But our Redeemer has not taught us a felfifh and tyrannical doctrine; he has not taught us to be fanguinary and oppreffive, nor to believe what the worthy fathers of the church, the beloved Jefuits, thofe Janiffaries of the Holy See, as Pope Benedict the Fourteenth emphatically called them, would have us believe, namely, that as often as they vociferate this maxim, that no heretic fhould be fpared, the found afcends to the throne of God, and is a pleafing oblation in his ear. It was not from the love of the religion of Jefus that the Spaniards fubjugated America, although under this pretext they depopulated a fpace of country as large as Europe, and put twelve or fifteen millions of the inhabitants to death, whofe only crime was the being in poffeffion of gold and filver, which the Spaniards coveted, and which they even offered to fhare with them; and although, with the moft inconceivable gravity, the Spaniards entered into an engagement at Hifpaniola to hang daily in cold blood, in

honour

honour of our Lord and his twelve Apoſtles, thirteen of the charitable Indians who brought them their daily food.

Religious pride is the cauſe of that theological rage with which Chriſtians of all ſects zealouſly labour for the good of their church, defend its doctrines with clamour and ſcurrility, and burſt out in triumph when erroneous or oppoſite opinions have been ably combated, or the embracers of them converted; and when they have given theſe notorious proofs of their attachment to their perſuaſion, they think themſelves real and zealous Chriſtians. But a great genius of our days, Dr. Reſewitz, profeſſor at Copenhagen, pertinently aſks, whether they ſhew as much earneſtneſs againſt the ſins the goſpel has prohibited to us, as they do in combating theological errors? Whether it is not often manifeſt that on other occaſions, when diſputation is out of the queſtion, they are indifferent to the moſt material points of Chriſtianity? Whether they do not quietly behold, or rather ſtudiouſly and deſignedly cloſe their eyes, when they are witneſſes of very great iniquity, and when the doctrine of Chriſt is more diſgraced by the manners of its followers, than by any ſpeculative errors that can ariſe? Whether they do not follow the mandates of their own wicked luſts with the ſame warmth with which they are

animated

animated in the purfuit and perfecution of mif-taken opinions?

In confequence of the prevalence of anathe-mas in Italy, whoever is guilty of an infraction of the laws of the church in the mereft trifles, is reckoned a far greater delinquent than the man who has committed the moft flagrant violations of the laws of nature and morality. A murderer, an adulterer, will more eafily gain his pardon of the church, and will more readily be readmitted into fociety, than he who has facrilegioufly dared to eat a bit of pigeon on a Saturday without an ex-prefs indulgence: the former is handled as gently and cautioufly as a nun does her confcience, when the fins of incontinency rife up againft her; but the latter is a monfter, a man whofe converfation muft be avoided, for he is nearly efteemed an heretic; and of all the fins of the Italian confeffion, herefy is the moft abhorred and damnable.

The contempt and hatred which prevail fo much between the oppofite perfuafions of the Chriftian religion, are alfo wholly confequences of the pre-judices occafioned by a bad education. The Chrif-tian youth are taught to condemn, what in their riper years they feel inclined to excufe; the poifon-ous feeds of hatred, difcord, and abhorrence are fown in their tender bofoms; and they learn at
school

school to deteſt as idolaters, or execrate as heretics, thoſe who, at the age of reaſon, they are tempted to embrace as brethren and fellow, Chriſtians. The more we attain to a found underſtanding of the real ſcope of the Chriſtian religion, the more we muſt feel the great abſurdity and narrowneſs of the prepoſſeſſions entertained by weak-minded Proteſtants againſt the members of the Roman church, or thoſe, on the other hand, which fooliſh Catholics cheriſh againſt the Proteſtants. The common people among us are wont to be mightily aſtoniſhed, when they hear of any generous deed of a Catholic towards a Proteſtant, or that the greateſt eſteem and friendſhip, together with the ſincereſt urbanity can exiſt between men of different religions. The inhabitants of Touloufe believed that it was an eſtabliſhed law among the reformed, that ſuch of them as abandoned their perſuaſion to embrace the Roman Catholic religion were to be ſtrangled; and, prepoſſeſſed with this idea, the Parliament of Toulouſe ordered the old and innocent Calas to be broke on the wheel, becauſe he was an Huguenot, and his ſon in a fit of melancholy hung himſelf without ever thinking of a change of religion. We muſt, unfortunately, when our reaſon is come to maturity, be very retentive of prejudices learned often by rote, and adopted without conſideration in our youth, if we do not ſee that it is poſſible to be true to our religion, without at the ſame time

being

being furprifed that others can likewife be true to theirs; that there is nothing fo rational and conciliatory as a perfect liberty of opinion; that, in a world where error and not truth is the portion of the greateft part of its inhabitants, God will judge our hearts, and not our underftandings; that we are all children of one common father, and coheirs of all his promifes, if we believe only as much as we can, and live according to his commandments ; and that virtue and piety, whether feen counting of beads and repeating the Ave Maria, or fitting down with a proteftant to a dinner of flefh-meat in lent, are always equally lovely and amiable *.

Let us now caft a few glances at other national follies. Men might often enjoy greater freedom were it not their own fault, but they fetter themfelves, and ftill, boafting of their liberty, are truly ridiculous. The conftitution of a country or a city may be free, and remain fo, and yet the minds of its inhabitants be in chains. Whoever in a republic acts folely on his own behalf, and fpeaks his mind freely only where he fees it can in no degree hurt either himfelf or his family, is very often againft his will and his confcience, and contrary to his oath and duty, an abject flave. The patriot inhabitants of a republican city ought therefore not to glory too much in their liberty, when the majority of

* The French tranflator has omitted this whole paffage.

them

them are ready, like fo many wild cats, to fly in the face of a ftranger, who fhould venture to affirm in public, that it is poffible for a burgomafter's fon to err in matters of literature.

The haughty prefumption of fole or pre-eminent courage, power, and confideration, is the caufe of the very aftonifhing perverfenefs of opinion prevalent in a nation with regard to all others, and an inexhauftible fountain of patriotic falfehoods for their hiftorians.. Few writers of hiftory guard themfelves fufficiently againft conceit and partiality, fhewing us the noble deeds of our countrymen, and the advantages gained by our own nation through a magnifying glafs, and thofe which may have been obtained over us by others through a very contrary medium.

The pride which proceeds from an ignorance of foreign affairs, deprives a nation of many advantages which flow from an acquaintance with the inventions and knowledge of other nations. Armed with impenetrable prejudices againft every ufeful innovation, it fixes its regard folely and liftlefsly on the foil it treads on, and thereby remains for ever enthralled by political fuperftition, which cleaves to the barren pride of anceftral worth, and condemns whatever is without precedent, however good in itfelf.

The pride that is founded upon ignorance, is the fureſt way to confirm our ignorance. Whenever we believe that we know all that is uſeful, there can be nothing elſe worth knowing; the arts and ſciences always will remain *in ſtatu quo* in every nation which fancies it is as far advanced in them as poſſible. This fooliſh perverſeneſs is a great hinderance to the extenſion of knowledge in many countries, which are otherwiſe very capable of improvement. The French defended and maintained the opinions of Deſcartes, long after his vortices, his elements, his theory of light, his romance of the formation of mankind, and all his other theoretic dreams, were confuted. Their national pride kept them blind to the power of attraction and the diviſion of the ſun-beams, as well as to the circulation of the blood, and the utility of inoculation, for an equal length of time; and they certainly would not have attempted the defence of the ſyſtem of Deſcartes after it had been exploded, if they were not addicted to the bad cuſtom of exalting every thing that is French, above all the inventions and diſcoveries made elſewhere.

But we are at preſent upon the eve of a great revolution, at the period of a ſecond demarcation between light and darkneſs. We may obſerve in Europe a ſecond general inſurrection in favour of good ſenſe and ſound judgment; the clouds of

ignorance

ignorance and fear are difpelling; weary of our long continued flavery, we are loofening the chains of ancient prejudices, in order to refume the poffeffion of our loft rights of common fenfe and ·freedom. The lights which are fo generally fpread abroad, the fpirit of philofophical inquiry which fo univerfally prevails, the great difcoveries it has made of the defects and errors of hitherto generally received opinions, and in fhort, the ftorming of the feemingly impregnable fortreffes of prejudice and ignorance, which have to this time kept us in fubjection; all manifeft a ftrength of thought, a hardinefs of intellect, which, though it often may fhoot out into a reprehenfible audacity, and will take from many the little fhare of liberty they poffefs, and the whole temporal welfare of more, as well as now and then a head or two, though it often will give occafion for fophiftry and fallacious fubtility to become the logic of the day; yet joined to manly policy, and a due deference to the laws, promifes to make our age that of the greateft improvements, and to give the mortal ftroke to barbarifm and fuperftition. The ufeful part of knowledge is no more made a fecret in the hands of a few pedants; the thinking part of every nation communicate their ideas to the public in the vernacular tongue, and the moft abftracted truths are now rendered comprehenfible, and brought home to the meaneft capacities. All the great interefts of mankind are confidered and

animad-

animadverted upon in writings of fenfe and feeling, which touch the heart and enlighten the under-ftanding; every thing is narrowly infpected and accurately defined; all is bufinefs and activity, and all feems to announce a general reformation in the practical as well as the theoretical part of life : this advances in fome places with flow and unfufpected fteps, in others it emerges at once, like the fun from behind a cloud, and diffipates every obftruct-ing mift. Even in Vienna, and in all the Roman Catholic States of Germany, we fee the fpirit of phi-lofophy boldly venturing forth; we fee it furmount the ftrongeft barriers of idlenefs and ftupidity, and rifing victorious in places where the throne of fuperftition was encompaffed by the moft hideous clouds of darknefs, prejudice, and ignorance. Some years ago, a man of learning came from a foreign country to Switzerland, intending to fettle in a land of liberty of opinion; he refided ten days at Zurich, and then left us to go even to Portugal.

Awake and read, is the beft aphorifm for the cure of prepoffeffion againft nations whom we do not fufficiently know; the more we converfe or correfpond with one another, the lefs will be our reciprocal contempt. Knowledge produces be-tween nations who have the moft rooted averfion for each other, a fpirit of amity and love; leffens that mutual national hatred, which cramps the foul;

deftroys

destroys the barriers of self-interest and jealousy, and, together with an extension of intellect, and a more manly elevation of mind, gives a greater degree of moderation and equity to our judgment of other nations. The learned are all members of the republic of letters, in which, notwithstanding the great inequality which is found in it, no tyrant is allowed nor any oligarchy permitted.

About forty years ago, a stranger, who might have had the impudence to let slip any mention of an English tragedy or comedy in good company at Paris, would have been hissed and hooted at. But now the most sensible Frenchmen allow, that to these bold Islanders we owe the present reigning and judicious system of morality and policy; that they first laboured for the advantage of the many and the interest of the nation; while in France nothing was thought of but wit and frivolity*: in a word, that the English possess as much genius, more energy, and only a little less taste than themselves.

Good English translations of some German writings would at once remove the greatest part of that contempt which the English writers entertain for

* The French translator has, instead of wit and frivolity, " que des ouvrages d'esprit."

I   the

the Germans. The time will come, when France will not reproach the Swifs, that a poet among them is as rare an animal and as great a wonder as an Elephant at Paris. It is not unlikely that in England, even now, a Swifs may be fuppofed to be endowed with the capacity of thinking; but the opinion of our intellectual abilities is generally formed from thofe ages of devotion and ftrict attention to propriety, when the firft public ftews were eftablifhed in Bern; and when at the fame time the caterpillars, which in 1479 had committed great ravages in our Canton, were by the patriotic counfel of the Apoftolical Doctor and City Recorder of Bern, Thuring Frikart, fummoned by a formal notification, to appear before the Spiritual Court of the Bifhop of Laufanne, who in conjunction with his ecclefiaftical Counfellors, after a due attention and accurate inveftigation of the complaint and defence, the reply and rejoinder, anathematized thefe caterpillars in the name of the Holy Trinity.

Even in Spain, formerly and yet the feat of credulity and fuperftition, a beginning has been made to command refpect, by a found difcuffion of the moft critical points of belief. Father Ifla, a Spanifh Jefuit, wrote a few years ago a novel under the title of the Hiftory of the highly famous preacher Gerundio of Campazas, furnamed Sotos (i. e. Dunderhead). The reverend brother Gerundio ap-

pears

pears as an epitome of all the extravagances, follies, and holy abfurdities, fo ufual in the Spanifh pulpits. It met with the greateft fuccefs; for the whole edition of the firft volume was fold at Madrid in the fpace of four and twenty hours, and the author afterwards fell into great penury, which is a fure proof that the nation thought well of his work,

The more fenfible part of mankind feems from time to time to adhere lefs to thofe opinions which keep them afunder, than to thofe which draw them together. The toleration of oppofite religions, becomes daily more advifable and more practifed by princes; and the more money is fpent at court, the greater complacency is ufed towards all improvements in philofophy and humanity; fince they all ferve to encreafe the income of the chamberlain *. The laws in England are fo mild with refpect to catholics, that they are fuffered to have their chapels, their fchools, and their priefts, together with the liberty of making profelytes, and likewife much influence in the parliamentary elections. The Elector of Mentz founded a fhort time ago a theological college of the Augfburgh confeffion in Erfurt. In Rome, ftrangers of all religions have for a long time been tolerated; for the fake of the

---

* This relates chiefly to Germany, where books are licenfed, and patents are granted by the chamberlains.

money they fpend, without being at all difturbed
on account of their faith, or being ever required to
join in any act of devotion of the Romifh Church.
The people, who in this refpect think exactly as his
Holinefs, only fay with a fmile, thefe folks are fo
unfortunate as not to believe in God. In Nice,
even where the believing populace is the moft
ignorant and ftupid of any in the catholic countries, it is a fact, that the moft fcrupulous Pied-
montefe farmer pays dearer for the dung which he
gets from the houfe of a proteftant, where flefh is
eaten every day, than for that of an honeft catholic, who muft put up with meagre diet one half
of the year; and as to the manure yielded by the
Reverend Fathers, the Minims, for that he will not
give a farthing. Controverfy is, in our times, quite
an uncultivated field, fince there now are proteftants
who have directly maintained, that all the moft
acute fyftems of polemical divinity are nothing but
a collection of reveries, and catholics, who can
forgive a proteftant, if otherwife an honeft man,
who does not hold as a geometrical truth that Saint
Michael reads mafs everymonday in heaven.

Over-weening national prejudices have likewife
partly fubfided, fince nations have infifted lefs
upon falfe points of honour. A very laughable circumftance in the hiftory of my own
country will illuftrate this truth to the reader,

if

if he compares the notion of honour then entertained by the Swifs with that we now hold.
In the year 1458, the Confederates were invited
by the city of Conftance to a fhooting party; but
unfortunately, near the conclufion of the diver-
fion, a Lucerner and a burgher of Conftance, being
about to fhoot for a wager, the Lucerner ftaked a
fmall piece of money coined in Bern, which is called
a *Plappert;* this the other in derifion called a *Kuh-
plappert* (that is, a piece of cow dung). This was
taken fo ill, that the Canton of Lucern immediately
urged the whole Confederacy to join them in refent-
ing the injury. The forces of the ftate affronted,
the honour-loving Lucern, aided by thofe of Under-
wald, opened the campaign by the invafion of
Thurgaw. They feized on Weinfeld, becaufe the
proprietor of that place was a near relation of the
aggreffor, and laid a contribution on the inhabitants of two thoufand florins. The other Confederates prepared likewife for war; the forces of
the Canton of Bern were already on foot, and
arms were not laid down till the city of Conftance reftored their pitiful honour to the Swifs
by a penitentiary gift of three thoufand Rhenifh
florins.

In our more enlightened days, nations will not
fo lightly attack each other from fuch miftaken
notions of honour; at leaft, as long as intereft is
the

the band that holds them together. Yet Newton will often be called an almanac-maker, and Montesquieu a blockhead, while the French and English struggle with all their power for the maſtery of the American trade.

The moſt inordinate pride muſt always accompany the moſt profound ignorance; for none but an empty Pariſian would ſuppoſe that his fellow citizens were the only thinking beings on earth; and none but a Spaniſh Eulogiſt of Saint Roche, would exclaim from the pulpit, in a complaining tone, " How could gracious Heaven permit ſo exemplary, ſo great a Saint, to be born a Frenchman !"

CHAPTER THE ELEVENTH.

OF PRIDE GROUNDED ON REAL ADVANTAGES.

THIS pride confifts in a confcioufnefs of the excellencies we in reality poffefs, and a due eftimation of them in confequence,

I need not make ufe of ingenious arguments to prove, that the pride we are about to treat of is effentially different from prefumption or arrogance. It is true, both individuals and nations may in one refpect be proud, and in another prefumptuous or vain; yet, pride is frequently feen unaccompanied by prefumption or vanity, and thefe again, often exift independant and unconnected with pride. In the latter cafe, it is from ideal advantages that arrogance is formed, and fuch real advantages as might rationally be expected to produce pride, are contemned and defpifed; whereas, in the former, a value is only placed on what is really valuable. Arrogance is vain of little advantages; pride of great ones. Arrogance ftrives for the pre-eminence every where and in every thing; pride

leaves

leaves fools to enjoy their own rank. Arrogance makes a man endeavour to be remarkable by his table, clothes, equipage, liveries, &c.; pride makes him truft folely to his own defert. Arrogance acts by miftaken notions of the point of honour; pride, by the principles of genuine honour. Arrogance is fond of fhewing its lordlinefs to inferiors; pride prefers to juftle with fuperiors. Arrogance is offenfive on account of its folly; pride, on account of its underftanding and virtue. Arrogance can defcend to every bafenefs; pride does not eafily ftoop to be mean. Arrogance often begets oftentation; pride, by a little turn of the fcale, becomes vanity. Arrogance is in every fhape folly; pride becomes folly when it gives way to felf-conceit, when it courts efteem and honours, when it exacts as a tribute from the world that praife which muft be a voluntary gift, or when it fecks for recompence immediately around itfelf, requiring it from every one near, and is impatient and peevifh at the leaft delay.

In the pulpit, pride is declaimed againft and rejected without exception, often indeed without reafon, and confequently without effect; although, on the other hand, two of the beft preachers, Spalding and Sterne, have inveighed againft it with the moft impreffive energy. But my object, as may eafily be feen, is not to depict

men

men as they fhould be, but as they are; and my chief aim is to exhibit the different ramifications of pride as they appear in man; to examine his nature in order to develope its caufes; to particularize and arrange the feveral appearances of pride as they occur; and to explain their refpective effects. From this inveftigation it plainly appears, that there are two forts of pride, and many fubdivifions belonging to each fort; that therefore the moral philofopher muft take care not to confound thefe two fpecies as in general is done; and that the language which cannot exprefs the confcioufnefs of real worth, in contradiftinction to the conceit of ideal advantages, or felf-efteem oppofed to felf-conceit, muft be barren indeed.

This confcioufnefs is effentially inherent in the nature of man, although it never has fair play; fince felf-love ever prevents us from eftimating our own advantages by the rule of equity.

In the minds of individuals, it is the fenfe of inward worth that Pythagoras held to be the greateft incentive to virtue; a centinel which the author of nature has placed within us, to keep aloof all that is little, mean, and unworthy the greatnefs of our foul; and, what requires to be particularly attended to, it is a perpetual exhorter to root out our defects. No bafe, malignant, or criminal thoughts will arife in

us,

us, if we entertain an esteem for ourselves, if we
submit all the inclinations of our soul to the tribunal of our judgment, and if we more fear our
own condemnation than that of others. The sense
of the beauty and dignity of human nature, to
which all moral virtue finally tends, seems not able
to subsist without this respect for ourselves. Im-
pressed with this sense of his own worth, a man
cannot avoid esteeming and valuing himself, but
only inasmuch as he makes a part of the community or nation over whom this noble sentiment
extends. The esteem for one's self is a curb to all
crimes ; a libertine clergyman is addressed, " Remember your ecclesiastical dignity ;" a magistrate,
who judges of the propriety of a complaint in proportion to the greatness of the sum of money which
accompanies it, is reminded, " That he sits in the seat
of justice." In the last war, when batteries upon
batteries, when two, three, and four successive en-
trenchments were to be forced, the cry was general
throughout the ranks of the assailants, " Remember
ye are Prussians :" in like manner, the vicious
should be called on, " Remember the high destina-
tion of man."

The consciousness of the real worth of one's
nation, is the same with national pride founded
on real advantages ; and this pride is a political
virtue of no small importance. The sense of the
worth

worth of our anceſtors, is a ſpur to emulation. Partaking in the fame of our nation for arts and ſciences, we are awakened to the deſire of encreaſing it. The conviction that we live under a good govern- ment, endears our country to us and ſecures our fidelity. The juſt pride of a nation, therefore, ariſes chiefly from its domeſtic advantages, but not always from the eſtimation theſe are held in by other nations. This eſteem is fought after by vain nations; and is but little valued by thoſe who are free; the Engliſh are not vain, for they do not care what others think of them; when honour is their motive for action, they do not take this mo- tive from the judgment of others; it ſuffices if they are eſtimable in their own eyes, or at moſt in thoſe of their countrymen. Yet vanity is ſo far con- nected with this kind of pride, inaſmuch as we believe our national fame exalts us individually in the eyes of foreigners.

The pride, therefore, that ariſes from real advan- tages, if kept within proper bounds, may be the germ of the greateſt elevation of mind. A man, who is wholly diffident of himſelf, or who by a due ſelf-eſteem does not poſſeſs a noble confidence in his own ſtrength, is unable to reſiſt common occurrences, and therefore incapable of any great action; he who has not the capacity of appreci- ating his own qualities, will ſeldom become an

objeſt

object of general efteem. It is only the man who
is confcious how far and wherefore he is eftimable,
and who never lofes fight of the calm benevolence
towards others which proceeds from modeft worth,
that can have a high fenfe of the dignity of human
nature. The beft founded pride is debafed to the
duft, if it endeavours to make contemptible what is
not fo: the beft founded felf-efteem is infufferable
when. it denies to others their due meafure of
refpect. Envy, too, can never accompany a proper
and noble pride, although it in nowife proceeds
from contempt; and, notwithftanding it affiduoufly
endeavours to fix contempt on its object, for it only
betrays a fear of being furpaffed. A noble mind
always feels gratified by the confideration of the
worth of others, which gives it a better fenfe of its
own greatnefs, in proportion as that of others is
more preceptible. Real merit is always difpofed to
emulation, never to envy or jealoufy. None but
men of very moderate underftanding will turn
away with difguft, from the contemplation of any
thing that bears the ftamp of perfection. A man
of fenfe never defpifes an ideot, for he knows but
too well how often he is like him; yet, he defpifes
the fool who endeavours to be of confequence, and
boafts when he is an ideot. The virtuous man
hates vice, but does not hate the vicious whom
he defpifes. Modefty is the moft attractive embellifhment of female beauty; but a woman of
exalted

exalted fentiments, who poffeffes the noble pride of confcious worth, which efteems itfelf, and has a juft claim to be efteemed by others, will defpife a heart that is infenfible to her real value, and which loves her more for her perfonal charms than for her mental excellencies.

But I am now led to the contemplation of the noble felf-efteem, which whole nations are poffeffed of; a profpect of greater extent, and requiring a more elevated tone, than the confideration of individual pride, already treated of.

L

CHAPTER THE TWELFTH,

OF PRIDE WHICH IS PRODUCED IN A NATION BY THE
REMEMBRANCE OF THE HEROISM AND VALOUR
OF ITS ANCESTORS.

Glowing representations and animated descriptions of the noble exploits and dangerous enterprizes which have been achieved by great men for their country's dearest rights, inspire the most distant generations with a generous pride of ancestral worth, and secure the lasting duration of that heroism which had become hereditary, giving magnanimity even to the effeminate.

The remembrance of the valour which encircled the brows of our ancestors with never-fading laurels, is a perpetual memorial and an unceasing incitement to us, that we should do nothing unworthy of their name; that we should esteem ourselves able to maintain it in all its pristine lustre. If we would imitate the virtues of our progenitors, if we would approach near to their renown, if we would revive their great and glorious days, we must be mindful of our origin, and of the duties it imposes on us;

we

we muſt keep our anceſtors in view, as our bright
examples; their deeds of hardihood and virtue
muſt be the favourite ſubjeẻts of our ſculptor's
and our painter's art, an animating fire enlivening
the ready eloquence of our orators, and the ſublime
imaginations of our poets: we muſt never look on
their renown as an inheritance, which we may enjoy in indolence; never indulge in that impatient
and jealous pride, which ſuggeſts that all muſt
yield to a name of glory, and which is irritated at
the preference preſent merit obtains over former
worth. It is then that our fathers live' again in
their deſcendants: the ſpirits of the great and
mighty ſlain beckon us to the battle; the moſs-
grown cenotaphs and ancient trophies ſeem to riſe
before us; the guardian Genii of our nation are ſeen
ſupporting in the air the ſhades of the illuſtrious
founders of our fame; and, enraptured by this
pleaſing viſion, even the vanity and frivolity of
vulgar minds yield to the thirſt of glory: every
heart and hand is united in the ardent purſuit of
honour; and every ſoul blazes with true patriotiſm,
and an undiſſembled admiration of our country's
virtue.

The ancients emulouſly encouraged one another,
by the remembrance of the heroic deeds of their
anceſtors,—to vigilance in peaceful times, and to
intrepidity in the hour of danger.—The noble ſentiments

ments of the Corinthians, on this subject, are thus expressed by Thucidides: " Your fathers have ascended to fame through rugged, steep, and untrodden paths; let their examples be ever present to you : do not lose by wealth and indolence, what labour and poverty has attained." All were exhorted not to remain inactively listening to the ancient stories, recounted by every nation, of their former advantages, for these are only honourable to those who strive to emulate them, and act only as a foil to the disgrace of those who recede from ancestral worth, since it is more unpardonable to depart from the great examples we have before us, and ought to follow, than to remain insignificant and inactive, without any.

Every thing among the Greeks conduced to plant in their hearts the most heroic courage, by the remembrance of their ancestors, whose principles and sentiments were the spur to the noblest actions. By the view alone of the statues of Harmodius and Aristogiton, the detestation of tyranny was renewed in the hearts of the Athenians, and their gratitude to these courageous champions of their liberty was daily and hourly augmented. They instituted public funeral rites, in honour of those who died for their country; and a pile was erected three days before the completion of the ceremonies, on which the remains of the slain were

L 3 publicly

publicly expofed to view: and the commonwealth took charge of the maintenance and education of the children of thofe heroes, till they attained the age of puberty. The loweft Greeks were exalted to a level with their greateft chiefs by a glorious death; their memory was renewed by the moft folemn offerings to the lateft pofterity, and their images were placed next to thofe of the gods.

Animated with the fentiments thefe maxims infpired, the Greeks advanced to their enemies. They encouraged one another with the recital of the deeds that had rendered their name famous, before the fignal for battle was given, and invoked the departed fpirits of their great forefathers to witnefs their actions on that day, when, proud of the glory they inherited, and worthy of the name they had gained, they refolved either to conquer or die. This noble refolution banifhed fear from their hearts, and conducted them with erect and cheerful countenances, to the very face of death, in fearch of honourable danger. The battle of Marathon alone was for many ages afterwards productive of the noblest emulation of equalling their anceftors. On every great occafion they called to mind this fignal victory: "Remember the innumerable hoft of Perfians; remember our own invincible little troop," was fhouted on every fide. We few, we happy few, we band of brothers,

was

was re-echoed from rank to rank. The nervous eloquence of Demosthenes engraved thefe fentiments on the minds of the Athenians, excited their deteftation of the artful king who attempted to undermine the ftate his arms could not fubdue, inflamed every mind with the energetic love of liberty and his country, and ftimulated every breaft to great and heroic deeds. The Spartans took the field, animated by this fpirit of unconquerable attachment to freedom and their country; their armies were fmall, but victorious. Even the prefent defcendants of the Spartans are the moft courageous among the modern Greeks, and, under the defpotic fway of the Turks, enjoy fome remains of their priftine liberty. · It was in order to renew in the Greeks the memory of their glorious anceftors that Agefilaus, when he invaded Afia, embarked at Aulis, the port whence the fleets and armies of united Greece took their departure, to revenge the rape of Helen: and when Alexander landed on that continent, to undertake its conqueft, his firft care was to awaken in his Greeks the remembrance of their former victories over the Trojans. He repaired to Ilium, and vifited the graves of Ajax, of Achilles, and of the other heroes who fell before the walls of Troy: he paid the cuftomary honours to their manes; he celebrated with his attendants games and courfes at the tomb of Achilles, fprinkled it with oil and crowned it with

garlands.

garlands. " Happy youth," he exclaimed at the monument of Achilles, " happy, that in thy life thou wert bleſſed with a faithful friend, and a Homer to immortalize thy valour." Such an avidity for glory, diſplayed with ſuch maſterly art, rouſed the nobleſt ſentiments in every breaſt. Alexander ſought to be like Achilles, his ſoldiers like Alexander : and this continual emulation warmed their imaginations and raiſed their ſouls far above every terreſtrial thought.

" Remember ye are Romans," was the common exhortation of the generals of ancient Rome to their companions in arms : this ſhort harangue ſufficed to rouſe them to perſeverance and indefatigable ardour in the moſt difficult enterprizes, and to intrepidity and firmneſs in the moſt bloody engagements. Filled with the memory of the valour of their anceſtors, and impreſſed with an enthuſiaſtic perſuaſion of the future greatneſs of immortal Rome, as immutably decreed by the gods, and announced by ancient prophecies, they ſubjugated nations, and conquered the world by the powerful influence of their conviſtion of the ſuperior privileges and advantages which were the birthright of a Roman citizen.

The Arabians owe the liberty they ſtill retain, to their courage : the Turks have not been able to

ſubdue

fubdue them, it is now many centuries; they are even daily extending their conquefts. They have eftablifhed themfelves in many parts of Egypt, and neither pay tribute to the Ottoman Porte nor obey his commands; and it is the memory of their anceftors that feeds and nourifhes this energy of foul. They hear, from their earlieft youth, the deeds of their forefathers recited in their tents: Arabia refounds on every fide with martial fongs, commemorating thofe feats of glory; and among its inhabitants, the poet is equally renowned with the hero he celebrates. The poetic pictures of the valour and intrepidity which characterized the golden ages preceding that of Mahomet, are faid to poffefs the fame unadorned fublimity we fo much admire in the beft productions of the Grecian and Roman mufe.

Thefe feeds of heroifm took ftill deeper root in the more ftiff and rugged foil of northern regions. Thofe indigenous Scythian nations, who wandered from the banks of the Tanais to Scandinavia, in order to live in eafe and comfort, who brought Sweden, Norway, Ruffia, and Denmark under the dominion of a Scythian family; who infenfibly extended themfelves through all Germany, and who fucceffively overwhelmed with the horrors of war the flourifhing provinces of Gaul, Spain, and, finally,

finally, the whole of the Empire of the Weft, upon which they poured down like the thickening clouds of a thunder-ftorm, impelled by the tempeftuous blafts of their own northern winds: thefe, I fay, had the fame origin, the fame laws, the fame courage, the fame love of liberty, the fame attach-ment to the cuftoms and religion of their fore-fathers, and the fame contempt of death, founded upon the hope of future and eternal happinefs.

The cuftoms and inftitutions of thefe nations were calculated to animate their fons, by reminding them of the prowefs and hardihood of their ancef-tors. Thefe predominant qualities were held in the higheft eftimation among them, and the love of war was deeply rooted even in their religion. Their deified Odin, inftead of a pure and abftracted no-tion of God, introduced an entirely fenfual fyftem; he knew how to adapt the Wolupfo, which was to form the religious code of the Scythians, to the genius of the nation; his Heaven and his Hell were folely founded upon a fcale of comparative valour; his laws far exceed thofe of Sparta, for the forcible injunction of the greateft contempt of death; the laft gafp of their warriors on the field of battle was immediately connected with all thofe recompences which filled the whole of their imagi-nations, and fuppreffed the paffion of fear, not by

cool

cool reafoning, or barren logic, but by the irrefift-. ible impulfe of other more violent and oppofing paffions.

Odin perfuaded the Scandinavians that thofe who died like their fathers, with arms in their hands, would alone enjoy an happy immortality. To rufh on the fwords of the enemy, and immedi- ately to enter into the fruition of the promifed re- wards, were, according to his doctrine, two occur- rences which were immediately confecutive. He per- fuaded them, that their future felicity depended en- tirely on the fhedding of their blood; and, in confe- quence, that a fick man muft on his death-bed procure himfelf to be wounded, in order to appear bathed in his blood before his gods.   Odin himfelf acted up to his doctrine.   The faith that he had pro- pagated during a long and profperous life, he con- firmed by a voluntary death.   Apprehenfive of the ignominious approach of difeafe and infirmity, he refolved to expire as became a warrior. In a folemn affembly of the Swedes and Goths, he wounded himfelf in nine mortal places, haftening away (as he afferted with his dying voice) to prepare the feaft of heroes in the palace of the god of war. After his example, the Scandinavians fought the higheft pitch of happinefs and luxury in blood and death. " Our warriors," fay their poets, " fearch out death with fmiles, and embrace
it

it with tranfport; they are feen in the battle, with their hearts transfixed, falling, laughing, and dying." Lodbrog, a Northern chief, thus exults at the hour of his death: " What undefcribable and hitherto unfelt emotions of joy arife in my foul! I die! I hear Odin's voice that calls me; I fee the gates of his palace open, the lovely wantons, having their moft bewitching charms half revealed to view, trip lightly forth, and beckon me to the banquet; their azure zones heighten the dazzling whitenefs of their bofoms; they approach, and offer me the moft delicious nectar, in fkulls ftill moift with the blood of my enemies."

All other virtues were held inferior to that of courage by the Goths, who indeed defpifed every thing elfe; but moft of all oftentation and magnificence. Their women even learnt the ufe of arms. A princefs, who chaftifed the temerity of a lover by flaying him with her own hand, was a fubject of admiration. A young man could fcarcely hope to fucceed in his courtfhip, if he had not given public and unequivocal proofs of his courage. The fon of a king dared not refufe the combat, which their religion fanctioned, if proffered even by the meaneft peafant; fince, conformably to their notions, victory muft declare itfelf in favour of the man who fought for a juft caufe.

Thefe

Thefe opinions, thefe deeds, were tranfmitted to pofterity by the firft melodious warblings of the Scandinavian poets : thefe fongs were recited to the boys, that their youthful hearts might early imbibe the knowledge of thefe heroic actions, which they would afterwards be called upon to emulate. They begat, in the fouls of the auditors, thofe wonders I hope to fee renewed by the immortal verfes of the Tyrtæus of Brandenburgh, and which I wifh for, from the glowing numbers of his Swifs brother.

The ancient Germans caught the fame fpirit. Their youth fought honourable death, in the hope of being celebrated by their bards. The moft valiant among them, upon his deceafe, was advanced to the rank of a god; his children and pofterity enjoyed the privileges of princes; they received gifts, and a large tract of land was affigned them: thefe privileges and this property was theirs as long as they were not unworthy of the glory of their progenitor. The beauteous daughters of the Franks * beftowed their favours only on the brave warrior, and their judgment both of the merit and tendernefs of his love was founded upon the proofs he had given of his valour; he muft have taken prifoners, fcaled fome dangerous and well-defended

---

* A nation in Germania. The French tranflator has it, the lovely women of France, &c.

precipice,

precipice, driven the enemy from fome ftrong
entrenchment, ere he could hope to fucceed with
his miftrefs; for fhe would rather behold him a
breathlefs corpfe, than fafely returned to her difgraced by flight. Hence the harfh din of arms re-
founded throughout all Germany, and the banners of
renown waved over every tomb. Even now, every
patriot German treads, with inward emotions of
reverence, the ground where the folemn remains of
his illuftrious anceftors repofe in filence; and approaches, with awe, the foreft where their fame ftill
hovers round the ancient oaks.   ·

Could the nations of the North, educated in
thefe opinions, avoid that noble efteem of themfelves, which their laws, their religion, and their
bards fo forcibly infpired? If they have not inherited from their forefathers a fondnefs for fofter
and more civilized renown, yet they have inherited
the nobleft examples of manlinefs of foul, which
have been deeply impreffed on their ardently emu-
lative minds.

The pride arifing from the martial fame of their
anceftors, has always been the greateft fpur to
courage and activity among the moft valiant nations. The youthful warriors of the Huns were
animated by a fpecies of phrenzy, folely by liftening

ing to the vocal melody, which revived and perpetuated the great achievements of their anceftors; a martial ardour flafhed from their eyes;
they became impatient for battle, and the tears
of the old men expreffed their generous defpair,
that they could no longer partake the dangers
and glory of the field.

The Japanefe were formerly a warlike nation,
fond of military renown, and of attempting the
moft extended and hazardous enterprizes. Their
moft ancient families were diftinguifhed by a noble
and majeftic countenance, and all defpifed death
and danger. The pride arifing from the glorious
reputation of their anceftors was extended even to
their children; their mode of education tended to
imprint ideas of heroifm and valour in their tender
breafts; fongs of war and victory were the firft
founds that reached their ears. In their fchools,
they were exercifed in tranfcribing the legends
of their heroes, and the hiftories of their progenitors, who had voluntarily devoted themfelves to a glorious death.

It was this fame pride that in former ages impelled our Helvetians to trample upon the necks of
their oppreffors, after the longeft ftruggles, and amid
impending dangers. A handful of ruftics gained
them

them liberty. The memory of those ruftics glowed in the hearts of the brave Bernians at Laupen; their little band refolved not to die unworthy their Helvetian fame; they advanced to battle; crowned with vine leaves, they chaunted the noble deeds of the founders of their liberty, and difperfed their proudeft foes like chaff before the wind. The memory of thofe ruftics occafioned the defeat of the Auftrian army at Sembach: their numerous and well-appointed cavalry fled before the intrepidity of a few Helvetians; numbers and difcipline were defeated by ardent impetuofity, and the moft tremendous apparatus of war yielded to the attack of fickles and ploughfhares, in the hands of the fons of freedom. The memory of thofe ruftics filled the hearts of the twelve hundred brave Helvetians, who, not far from Bafle, attacked forty thoufand French, committed a great flaughter among them, and difputed the victory with unconquerable intrepidity, till the few remaining of their hardy troop were confumed to afhes among the ruins of a church, into which they had retreated and which was fet on fire, they having refufed to furrender. The memory of thofe ruftics inflamed the fouls of our fathers, who, at Murten, drove the Burgundians before them, as the light fand of the defert before the fierce Typhon and Ecnephia. The memory of thofe
ruftics,

ruftics, gained, by a thoufand immortal actions, before their pofterity was degenerated, the confidence of princes, the admiration of Europe, an eftablifhed peace, and handed down to us for a lafting inheritance, only that Noftalgia * which death alone can deprive us of.

-The pride, therefore, that arifes in a nation from the glorious reputation and known valour of their anceftors, is an abundant fource of inflexible greatnefs of foul, and the moft certain prefervative againft the pernicious effects of pufillanimity.

* This is a difeafe almoft peculiar to the Swifs. It is a vehement longing after one's native country when abfent from home.

M

CHAPTER THE THIRTEENTH.

OF PRIDE ARISING IN A NATION, FROM THE REPUTA-
TION ACQUIRED BY ARTS AND SCIENCES.

By the pride above defcribed, I underftand that noble felf-efteem which a nation poffeffes from the opinion of its fuperior talents, either as derived from their progenitors, or from their own exertions.

This felf-efteem is a natural confequence of the high opinion entertained of arts and fciences, and of their power over the human heart: it is in faƈt by their influence that the powers of the foul are unfolded, that the circle of its operations are enlarged, its comprehenfive faculties encreafed, and every fpark of latent genius called into aƈtion. A man of an enlightened underftanding perceives with eafe the vulgar errors of mankind, the prejudiced and vain-glorious ideas of all ages; he alone is able to judge of the wifdom, propriety, truth, and beauty of any fentiment or aƈtion. Similar to a being looking down from the Empyrean on this world, he beholds with compofure,

pofure, from his unclouded height, the mafs of mankind yet wandering in darknefs and error, their miftakes and deviations, and the gloomy tempefts that rage in the deep glens below him. The fciences collectively teach the foul duly to appreciate its own greatnefs, and fill it with difguft for the fanguinary laurels of military fame. Darius was already vanquifhed, and Afia fubjugated, when Alexander wrote to his preceptor Ariftotle, that he had much rather be exalted above all mortals by fuperior knowledge, than by the magnitude of his power; and in Corinth, he had long before declared, that if he were not Alexander, he fhould choofe to be Diogenes.

This noble fentiment is felt by a whole nation, when it has produced a number of eminent men. The memory of thofe worthies who lived for their country, is as dear to well informed minds as that of the heroes who died for their country. Every nation is proud of its learned men, its philofophers, and its artifts, as foon as they have paid their tribute to envy by their death; for thofe nations who are moft vain of their great men when dead, are often the moft backward to acknowledge their worth while living. It is only for thofe who lie mouldering in their graves, and who can no more be objects of jealoufy, to enjoy a reputation which envy cannot harm; and with thefe limitations we

may

may fay that the fame of a nation in fciences, proceeds from the fame of fome of its individuals, according to the meafure of the genius and the ideas of all its members.

Thofe who have enlightened their country by their talents, who have ftrengthened it by their philofophy, and adorned it by their genius, are, if I may be allowed the expreffion, Atlafes, who fupport the name and dignity of their nation, and tranfmit them unimpaired to future ages. Their nobleft part lives and is active when they are no more; and their names and knowledge, fnatched from oblivion by their writings, are legacies bequeathed to the whole world. We admire the impreffions of their expanded fouls, which appear in the memorials which they have left for our aftonifhment and inftruction; in them ftill breathes their genius; in them ftill burns the confecrated fire of patriotifm;' thence it has darted into the breafts of the great men who have fucceeded them; thence, even at this moment, perhaps, a fpark flies off, which may infufe new life into a whole exanimate pofterity; may awaken their regret for having loft the precious inheritance, and, by a contemplation of the fublime eminence whence they have fallen, inflame their hearts with a noble emulation of its grandeur.

M 3

The

The Greeks conceived, that for confolation in adverfity, deliverance from danger, the extenfion of their fame, and the luftre of their actions, they were folely indebted to their fages. In fact, many of the Athenians who fell into flavery by Nicias's unfortunate expedition againft Sicily, owed their prefervation to Euripides, whofe verfes they recited to their mafters; and in general their literati were fo famous, that a King of Perfia, when he admitted fome Grecian ambaffadors to an audience, firft of all enquired of them, how the Poet Ariftophanes did? Without the father of poetry, Achilles himfelf would have been buried in eternal oblivion. Raifed to the throne by courage and probity, and filled with the animating fpirit of Grecian knowledge, Ptolemy Philadelphus made his capital city of Alexandria the metropolitan feat of arts and fciences. He founded the mufeum, the moft ancient and moft fumptuous temple ever erected by any monarch, in honour of learning; he filled it with men of abilities, and made it an afylum for philofophers of all defcriptions, whofe doctrines were mifunderftood, and whofe perfons were perfecuted; in whofe unfeigned tribute of grateful praife, he has found a furer road to everlafting renown, than his haughty namelefs predeceffors, who pretended to immortality, and braved both heaven and corroding time by the folid ftructure of their

pyramids, .

pyramids, which have outlived the memory of their builders.

Rome arofe from conqueft to literature, from the knowledge of the worth of valour to the knowledge of the worth of the arts and fciences. The arms of this mighty people had indeed fubdued Greece, but Greece could prove to the Romans, that greatnefs of genius can exalt the flave above his mafter; and that fupereminence is attainable at a diftance from the feat of victory and the ruins of demolifhed thrones.

The fall of the republic feemed to fix the ftability of the empire of the arts. The world fubmitted to the abfolute fway of one, and, tired of war and flaughter, the tyrant Auguftus became a protector of the mufes. Virgil read his poetry to him in the imperial palace; the firft minifter of ftate was appointed to relieve him when he became tired of reading; overcome by his divine numbers, Octavia fwooned at his feet, and Auguftus was melted into tears. The Emperor chofe Horace for his favourite, but Horace had the courage to decline that honour. Rome, even in chains, was rendered great and illuftrious by its writers, whofe renown became that of the empire and its pride.

The

The admiration fo liberally beſtowed on their fellow citizens, who had exalted themſelves by the greatneſs of their genius, was the moſt fruitful nurſery for great men, both among the Greeks and the Romans. Athens had erected the buſts and ſtatues of its meritorious children in the Cerami-cus, and Greece was filled with the like monu-ments of deſert. Their renown aſſailed on every ſide minds which burnt with impatience to deſerve the ſame honours. The Roman youth, when they beheld the images of their illuſtrious anceſtors, ex-poſed in public on the celebration of certain ſolemn ceremonies, were ſo forcibly ſtruck with veneration for their virtues, that the graves ſeemed to open and the ſhades of the dead to appear on earth, in order to teach them, in the language of the immortals, the way to every thing great, ſublime, and praiſe-worthy.

A nation cannot be more powerfully impelled to the love of ſcience and of virtue, than when it con-templates domeſtic examples of them, with a noble pride of heart. Every nation ought to reſpect and eſteem thoſe by whom it has been enlightened and improved; it ought to reverence their images; to celebrate their memories; and all hearts ſhould glow with the deſire of being equally great and illuſtrious. The pride which ariſes in conſequence of the opinion of the ſuperiority of our talents

and

and knowledge above all other people, was accordingly peculiarly prevalent both among the Grecians
and the Romans.

Athens, even under Pericles, aftonifhed its neighbours by the mafter-pieces of its artifts and fages.
Pericles, who immortalized the memory of his
heroes by Phidias's art, who raifed the genius of
Attica to its higheft pitch of elevation by his unexampled eloquence, was the foul of Athens. It
is impoffible to perufe the travels of Paufanias
through this beautiful country, without being pene-
trated with the moft ardent admiration. We lif-
ten with rapture to the defcription of the many
mafter-pieces he enumerates ; every fpot of Greece
teemed with the moft exquifite productions of
architecture, fculpture, and painting, and the whole
in a manly and genuine elegance of tafte. Greece
produced for a long feries of ages great men of
every defcription, who, ftimulated by their creative
genius, deviated from the beaten track, and ftruck
out new and untried paths to immortality. All
their productions bore the ftamp of nature in its
greateft beauty, and glowed in the colours of truth.
Defpifing the common conveniences of life, they
travelled over the remoteft lands, to expand and
invigorate the powers of their minds. And the
veftiges which the Romans have left us of their
greatnefs, and of their defire of eternal fame, in all
                                                    the

the three continents of the ancient world, are not only monuments of their religious veneration for their great men, but at the fame time as many memorials of their own pride.

Italy, England, and France, approach in modern times the neareft to Greece and Rome, by the juft eftimation of their refpective merits in the arts and fciences.

The Italians are, with reafon, proud of the reputation of their nation in the arts and fciences. The Italian cities had fcarcely reared the ftandard of liberty, before the light which had previoufly illuminated Greece and Rome burft through the fhades of the Gothic chaos ; the flame of thefe revolutions vivified the arts and fciences, and produced immortal mafter-pieces of every kind. By the liberal employ of the riches, an extenfive commerce and flourifhing manufactures had brought to Florence, and impelled by that defire of fame which patronizes the operations of genius, and gives birth to the nobleft defigns and actions, this city ftrove for the attainment of every fpecies of renown. Europe beheld patriotifm, found policy, and military fame, regenerated together with the arts and fciences, the fources of which had fo long been dried up during the barbarous ignorance of the middle ages. Florence was before and under the

Medici

Medici what Athens was in the zenith of its glory. Italy, prieftly Italy, was of all the European ftates the firft where the fine arts were cultivated, pro- tected, encouraged, and rewarded. From that country were emitted the firft fparks which an- nounced and kindled the brighteft flame of return- ing knowledge. A Francifcan monk, advanced to the papal throne, Sextus the Fifth, contributed more to the embellifhment of Rome in his fhort pontificate of five years, than Auguftus, the lord and mafter of the riches of the world, in a reign of forty. From Italy came thofe fciences which have fince produced fuch abundant fruits in the reft of Europe; to her we are in particular in- debted for the fine arts, and it is from her nume- rous inimitable productions, that we owe the good tafte now fo univerfally diffufed among us.

The veneration of the Italians for great men effentially contributed to their formation. Florence is crouded with monuments erected to perpetuate their fame, both by the fovereigns and private individuals of the country. The houfe built by the celebrated Viviani very near Santa Maria Novella, exhibits a ftriking mark of his gratitude towards the famous Gailileo, whofe difciple he always called himfelf; the front of the houfe is decorated with the ftatue in bronze of this renovator of one of the moft fublime fciences; and on the pannels, between the windows, are infcribed the dates and particular defcriptions of thofe difcoveries with which Gallileo enriched the magazine of know-ledge.

The efteem of the Florentines for thefe monu-ments erected during the fine age of the arts is fo great, that they hold it a kind of facrilege even to clean, fcrape, and polifh thofe images, which, ftanding in the open air, generally undergo an ab-lution in the fpring. The hundred and fixty public ftatues, which ftrike the eye of a ftranger, and attract his notice as much as the fineft ornaments of the moft flourifhing city of Greece did Pau-fanias, are expofed to all the injuries of the weather, and entirely left to the care of the populace, who refpect them as facred relics. This refpect defcends from parent to child, and is founded on a tafte for the fublime and beautiful, which the habit of feeing fuch things admired and hearing them praifed ren-ders natural; and this habitual attachment to the fine arts is fo inherent in the Italians, that the ladies of Rome and Florence can difcourfe with as much propriety on the fubject, as ever a German profeffor did on the fcience he practifes.

The Florentines bear a ftriking fimilitude to the ancient Athenians, in the veneration they profefs for whatever has any relation to their country.

Florence

Florence is in their eyes with refpeƈt to the whole of Europe, what Athens in the famous panegyric of Ifocrates is reprefented to be with refpeƈt to all the reft of Greece.   They view in Florence every excellence of every kind and every age; and, in regarding other nations, owing to this felf-efteem, they behold nothing but barbarity and ignorance; they fancy that they alone have invented, produced, and praƈtifed every thing that is ufeful or agreeable.

Among other inconteftable inftances of the grofs ignorance of foreigners, the Florentines relate with great felf-complacency the following ftory of a Ruffian nobleman.   He was viewing the celebrated colleƈtion of Baron Stofch: "And this," faid his conduƈtor, " is the buft of my Lord."—"What, is the original fo antique?" rejoined the Ruffian, in the tone of a connoiffeur.   But nothing can exceed the conduƈt of the confeffor of Charles the Third of Spain, in the library of the Medici: this confeffor, a reformed Francifcan or Cordelier, accompanied the young prince when he went to take poffeffion of his Tufcan territories; being the only perfon in his fuite who bore any appearance of fcholarfhip in his drefs, the librarian prefuming his curiofity could be no better fatisfied than by the view of that fuperb colleƈtion of books, one of the moft brilliant memorials the munificence of princes had dedicated

to

to literature, immediately waited on him with a refpectful invitation to fee the library of the Medici. He accepted the invitation, and appointed a day; the librarian had affembled all the moft eminent literati of Florence, who being joined by the confeffor, he proceeded with this fplendid retinue towards the library. On coming to the door, he ftopped fhort, caft a vacant look round the faloon, and turning to the fuperintendant, faid, " Pray Mr. Librarian, have you got the book of the feven Trumpets here ?" The librarian replied, that it was not in the collection, and the whole learned company were obliged to confefs with fome confufion, that they were unacquainted with fuch a book; upon which the confeffor, turning his back upon the library, declared that the whole of it was not worth a fingle pipe of tobacco. It was afterwards difcovered, that this book of the feven Trumpets was a collection of the moft improbable devout ftories, wrote in Spanifh, by a Monk of the order of St. Francis, the tranflation whereof forms part of the contents of thofe books printed in France under the title of *Bibliotheque Bleue.*

But Italy, once the emprefs of the world, is now the fcene of defolation and rapine, and dependant upon thofe nations who were formerly her flaves; once the protectrefs of all arts and fciences, fhe is now reproached with flumbering over her faded laurels;

laurels; she is now again reduced to a state of insignificancy, from the height to which the founders of her modern fame, Gallileo and Columbus, had raised her; by the discovery of new worlds on earth by the latter, and in the heavens by the former; the seeds from which those truly great men sprung are yet in existence, but torpid and inactive, without a shoot, or without a single leaf of honour. The Italians have for near a century ceased to be like themselves. They have before their eyes master-pieces of art and models of good taste, examples of the talents of their ancestors; but these precious remains are an unprofitable heap to them, and neither kindle the fire of genius, nor incite the labouring hand of industry to emulation. We must not visit Italy for the sake of the Italians, but for the sake of the country they inhabit.

These reproaches, it is true, are carried rather too far, and are the more grating to the Italians, as there are few nations so sensible of the esteem of foreigners. Philosophy, mathematics, physics, natural history, the art of medicine, and the fine arts, are nearly as flourishing in Italy as in France or England. Most of the Italian universities make it their study to prevent the prostitution of the sublimest sciences, by the trite and dry application of them, to the injury of mankind, which has so long prevailed in the seminaries of monkish learning. Both the

nobility

nobility and the higher orders of the clergy think it not beneath them to rival one another in every fpecies of human knowledge ; while at the fame time, as well through the whole of Italy as at Rome, the common people are completely ignorant and unprincipled, and have no other opportunity for inftruction, than the very feldom occuring executions of malefactors.   The tafte for folid knowledge encreafes every day in Italy ; many of their authors write with freedom, and their ideas are not invariably fettered to ancient prejudices.   The modern Italian philofophers break the bands of hierarchy and defpotifm, with an almoft unexampled boldnefs.   We need only read the work of a noble Italian, on the reformation of Italy, the treatife on crimes and punifhments of the immortal Beccaria, the Coffee-houfe, an Italian weekly publication,   in comparifon with which the Englifh Spectator feems to be only written for women ; the reflections of an Italian on the church in general, on the regular and fecular clergy, and the head of the church ; and we fhall be afhamed of harbouring the thought that Italy is totally deprived of genius.

In all the fciences and almoft in all the arts, the Englifh are as eminent as men can be, and, as we may eafily perceive, are too confcious of their excellence. By the honours they confer on their meritorious
country-

countrymen, they give the moft convincing proof
how proud they are of their merit.

In no country of the world are rank, birth, and
every thing that is not perfonal, held fo effentially
different and diftinct from merit. In Germany, on
the appearance of a ftranger, the firft queftion is,
" whether he is a nobleman ?" in Holland, " has he
money?" but in England, "what fort of a man is he?"
In the reign of Henry the Eighth, a lord complained to the king of an affront he had fuffered
from the painter Holbein : " Let Holbein alone,"
faid the king, " for I can whenever I pleafe make
feven lords of feven plowmen, but I cannot make
one Holbein of even feven lords." A minifter
of ftate, in England, is a kind of intermediate
being, between an angel and the worft of the
human fpecies. The Earl of Chatham is deified
by fome, and ill-fpoken of by others, and yet
merit is no where elfe in the world fo juftly
appreciated as in England. This people, often
fo turbulent and unruly under the pretence of
liberty, forego hatred, enmity, fect, and party
when they are called upon to reward great talents.
Where the afhes of their kings repofe, there repofe
likewife thofe of their heroes, of their poets, and
of their men of genius of every defcription. The
remains of an actrefs, which in France have no
better receptacle than a dunghill, are interred in

England

England next to thofe of the greateft ftatefman.
Newton received in this nation, fertile in great men,
extraordinary honours when living, and after his
deceafe he was carried in regal pomp to this filent
repofitory, facred to the memory of monarchs and
departed genius. The honours fo liberally beftowed upon great talents in England, have in every
age induced the nobleft among its peers to interweave the bays with their coronets; and the moft
abftrufe difquifitions are as common in daily converfation there, as difputes concerning a new head-
drefs, or a fafhionable ragout in France.

The Englifh owe the greater degree of liberty
they enjoy above other nations, to the fuperiority of
their knowledge. Animated by a fpirit of freedom, of which no adequate idea can be formed,
even in moft republics, they faften upon the fciences as a tyger on its prey; they meditate on the
great interefts of nations, and of mankind, with
the moft daring expanfion of thought; they are
ever taken up with great objects, and ever doing
great things. Ignorance and error fhrink from
the penetrating vifion of their genius; arbitrary
power trembles before their vigorous inveftigation
of its principles, while the authority of the law
alone ftands immoveable and facred. The greateft
part of fuch nations as are free, think and act but
by halves; while on the other hand, the Englifh

foar with a steady flight to the skies, becaufe their wings are not clipped, neither are they called back by the lure of the falconer.

The merits of the French, with which they themfelves are well acquainted, very often burft forth with tranfcendent fplendour. We are too much accuftomed to fee them in a ridiculous point of view; whereas an eulogium upon them would be more eafily compofed than a fatire.

The prefent men of genius among them are fupereminently great. They feem at once adapted to every thing worthy the attention of man: they fcan the heavens, and poffefs the greateft refinement of fenfibility; they claim our admiration when they enlarge our ideas on the moft abftrufe fciences, and our tears when they charm us with an affecting narrative of misfortune; and all their writings poffefs the moft inimitable elegance. Order, method, and energetic perfpicuity are their own; every thing fuperfluous, low, or trivial is banifhed from their plan; every thought is placed in its moft advantageous light. Even when they fuperficially and lightly approach the outworks of fcience, they do it with fuch penetration, that they feem at every ftep to pierce into the deepeft fanctuaries of knowledge. They decide with dignity, and difpute with mildnefs; and above all other nations,

they

they poſſeſs the invaluable art of being both philoſophers and men of the world, ſtudying by the
midnight lamp, and at the ſame time avoiding
pedantry.

The French have in particular given the ſciences
an attic elegance. Their drama, conſidered altogether, ſurpaſſes that of every other modern nation;
and they have brought to greater perfection than
any other people, the moſt uſeful and moſt agreeable of all arts, that of good manners and ſocia-
bility; they have carried natural philoſophy, politics, commerce, finances, and the imitative arts to
their greateſt height.   The numerous inſtitutions
and rewards for learning of every kind in France
give it a ſtriking advantage, awakening diligence
and emulation; and, to theſe, France owes the
exalted degree of renown it has attained in aſtro-
nomy, and in tactics: philoſophy is advancing with
rapid ſtrides among them; all mankind at preſent
think on every thing, and the French as much as
any other nation. Did their great men not bow their
heads ſo low to a ſex, who highly prize whatever
is trifling, and ridicule whatever is truly great, to
a ſex, to whom we will gladly reſign the empire of
the heart, provided they leave us that of the mind,
ſtill more might be expected and derived from them.

There is another ſort of equitable ſelf-eſteem,
which ariſes from the awakening of a people to a
                                                    ſenſe

fenſe of their own natural advantages ; and though
the benefits which accrue from it are often ʼmiſ-
underſtood and cried down, it neverthelefs embraces, in my opinion, every thing that can be
called great and noble. I mean that ſpirit of
liberty which the writings of the Engliſh have
created and cheriſhed in the hearts of the French ;
and which inſtils into the ſoul of a Pariſian philoſopher, in his attic dwelling, on the ſeventh ſtory,
the juſt and neceſſary pride due to the true dignity
and freedom of his charaƈter as a citizen of the
world.* This ſpirit does honour to human nature,

---

* The French tranſlator has here as follows : `` Je parle de
l'eſprit de liberté que les chef-d'œuvres de l'Angleterre commu-
niquent aux François, & qui donne neceſſairement aux philoſophes
de la France le juſte orgueil qu' *autoriſe la dignité du gouvernement
fous lequel ils vivent.*'' `` I mean that ſpirit of liberty which the
writings of the Engliſh communicate to the French, and which
neceſſarily gives the philoſophers of France that juſt pride which
the dignity of the government under which they live authoriſes.''—
And a little lower down : `` Les Anglois regardent les François
comme un peuple d'eſclaves, tandis qu'ils font pour la plupart
aux pieds du thrône auſſi libres *que les Anglois, qui ſe piquent le
plus de jouir de cet avantage.*'' `` The Engliſh look upon the
French as a nation of ſlaves, while for the moſt part they are at
the foot of the throne as free *as the Engliſh, who pique themſelves
the moſt upon the poſſeſſion of this privilege.*'' The next ſentence
which relates to ſome of the writers of the Encyclopædia, he
omits wholly ; and the following paragraph throughout is equally
tranſlated with the ſame prejudice, betraying either an evident
fear of giving offence, or the groſſeſt partiality, highly injurious
to the province of tranſlation.

and

and adminifters confolation and encouragement to
depreffed humanity, while employed in removing,
with a tender but fteady hand, the film of prejudice
from the eyes of mankind.   The Englifh, prepof-
teroufly think the French are a nation of flaves;
but it is ridiculous to defpife them as flaves, for
there are many Frenchmen, even at the foot of the
throne, who have fouls as free as the freeft Englifhman; and there are fome of the writers of the
Encyclopædia who are more determined republicans than moft of the jurifts either in Holland
or in Switzerland, and they are publicly known to
be fuch, and are yet refpected.

Moft of the parliaments of France examine and
afcertain the true interefts of the nation and of
the king, with a noble and unfhackled eloquence;
they lay before the throne the bleffings and the
love of all ranks, in order to procure fecurity,
peace, and the hope of better days to the palaces
of the great, and the cottages of the poor.   Their
hearts are not caft down by oppreffion; their fouls are
capable of the greateft and nobleft fentiments; and
they are ready, at the rifk of their own eafe, of their
wealth, and of their places, undauntedly to utter the
voice of reafon and of truth.   This fpecies of liberty
confifts in the uncontrolled exercife of one's faculties;
it does not owe its origin to a form of government,
but to found judgment and philofophy; and is fo
much

much more laudable than that fpecies neceffarily
arifing from the political conftitution of a country,
in proportion as it has greater difficulties to furmount. A nation, therefore, may be juftly and
greatly proud of its liberty of opinion, when it does
think with freedom, and not becaufe it may.

The merit of individuals in the arts and fciences,
therefore, produces in a nation a very juftifiable
pride, which, as long as it is kept within proper limits,
elevates the mind, banifhes fuperftition and ancient
prejudices by the aid of philofophy and found judgment, and exalts the fpirit of liberty the more the
various principles and opinions of a nation are can-
vaffed and inveftigated.

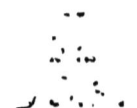

CHAPTER THE FOURTEENTH.

OF PRIDE PRODUCED IN A NATION BY ITS CONSTITUTION.

In the fame manner as we contemplate with awe, an auguft temple in its ruins, fo do we reverence that frame and conftitution of things, exifting in our peculiar country, even until the laft moments of liberty.

The pride that is produced in a nation by its frame of government, I define to be the fenfe of the high and pre-eminent value of its conftitution.   A wild, headftrong, lawlefs youth prefers a democratical government; a cunning and intriguing man, a monarchy; the felf-interefted, that government which infures the greateft perfonal profits to him felf; a noble and philanthropic foul, that under which the greateft number of men are rendered happy and profperous : but in general we may ob-ferve the moft deeply rooted, and, in my opinion, the beft founded pride, in thofe countries whofe inhabitants are moft fubordinate to duty, and leaft fo to each other; and where, for that reafon, as

much

much civil liberty may be found as is confiftent with the exiftence of fociety.

It is extremely difficult for every government to infpire its fubjects with a fenfe of its own peculiar excellence; but it is not difficult for fubjects to love the conftitution of their country; which always ought to be an object of refpect and vene-ration. A man of fenfe may find happinefs under every moderate government; one fpark of inward content is fufficient to embellifh all around him. We often fee complaints urged againft the beft governments; but we ought to confider, that the beneficial fruits of laws, and of the adminiftration of government, are in general invifible, and never immediately appa-rent; while, on the contrary, the fmalleft and moft unavoidable evils are inftantly perceptible, and are converted by exaggeration and mifrepre-fentation into the moft frightful phantoms to ap-pal the brainlefs populace.

We may be happy under the fhelter of civil liberty, both in republics and in monarchies; in the former, indeed, by right, in the latter by chance; and in fact, equally fo in every country where wholefome laws are the rules by which men are governed, or where the will of a juft and en-lightened prince is the fupreme law.

CHAPTER THE FIFTEENTH.

OF REPUBLICAN PRIDE.

In all republics we may find this pride; but I do not here allude to thofe in which republicans may in vain be looked for at mid-day with a candle and lanthorn.

I call a republican, the man in whom the love of freedom, of his country, and of the laws, together with the execration of defpotifm, are predominant. Others may give a very different definition; but, if mine fhould be the true one, it cannot be denied that there may be great and genuine republican fouls in monarchies, as well as abject and fervile ones in republics.

Pride in republics, is the confcioufnefs of the liberty, equality, and fecurity we enjoy under a republican government. Liberty is that ftate of mankind in which our actions, if they are juft, and founded upon rational principles, cannot be controlled by any external force. Our will to

perform,

perform, however, muft be fubject to our reafon, for we cannot will any thing without a motive. If a man, in this ftate of fociety, wills any thing that is bad, there is always a power withftanding him, which prevents the execution of his will, if he liftens to its dictates; but by this power he is not deprived of his civil liberty; for freedom, in a ftate of fociety, only allows us to fatisfy our real neceffities in an irreprehenfible manner; if in any ftate it allows of more, it degenerates into licentioufnefs: and this idea of liberty, is perfectly defcriptive of the fituation of a republican; he wills as long as his will is not repugnant to the laws.

Mules tread with a fure foot, along the brink of a precipice, and they are, therefore, in fuch places, left to their own guidance: but man is not fo fortunately gifted; for, without the reftraint of law, liberty could not exift in a ftate of fociety. The will is more frequently guided by the blindnefs of inftinct, than by the fober light of reafon; and the law itfelf is, therefore, often not fufficiently coercive to keep men within due bounds: on which account, it has been found neceffary in all republics, to confide in a number of citizens who have deferved well of their country, or are efteemed worthy to ferve it, the care of watching over the laws, of carrying them into execution, and of changing and new-modelling

them,

them, as a change of circumftances and times may require. Liberty, therefore, does not confift in having no power on earth fuperior to ourfelves, but in this fuperior power not exifting in the arbitrary will of one. Where this power refides in the abfolute will of many, there ought to be fuch provifions in the law, by which one will always be prevented from maftering or controlling the others: where there are fuch laws, the moft eminent man is but the firft fubject of the law; and wherever no one is exempt from its fway, none can be the flave of another.

Thofe conftitutions which are moft free, have always required the ftricteft obedience, becaufe freedom can only be fupported by the maintenance of the laws. In order to accuftom the people to fubmiffion to the law, in the moft trifling and indifferent matters, the Ephori of Sparta, on their entrance into office, had it proclaimed, by the found of a trumpet, that every Spartan fhould cut off his whifkers; for they were anxious to have all their laws obferved with the fame willingnefs and readinefs, as that which permitted a young fellow to afk leave of an old man, who might have a youthful wife, to beget him a child.

Hence, republican liberty leaves man in the poffeffion of his original rights, fo far as he can enjoy them compatibly with the rights of fociety. The
exemption

exemption from that miferable fate which makes man, funk from his inherent dignity, fubmit to be a flave, not indeed becaufe he wills, but becaufe he muft, ftrengthens the foul, expands the underftanding, and enlarges the ideas, giving to every faculty, fire, vigour, and energy. Pure liberty is only found in the noble bofom that abhors all chains, whether the golden ones of kings, or the iron ones of republics, which do not admit even a fuperficial gilding. Every free foul at court fighs after black bread and liberty. Here its all-vivifying energy produces a certain natural artlefs eloquence, on which depends the moft important civil and political concerns; as it is the moft proper inftrument, fometimes to appeafe the multitude, fometimes to roufe, often to convince, but oftener to perfuade. There its mild and benevolent power extends over philofophy, for thofe who entirely difrobe truth, muft of neceffity approach the neareft to it.

Equality is held to be the exclufive advantage of thofe republics, where every member of the commonwealth can arife to the firft dignities of the ftate; where their election depends upon the people in general; and where thofe dignities are not in any cafe hereditary. But the fyftem of abfolute moral equality among men is falfe and abfurd, becaufe fociety can only efteem a man according to the probable proportion of his ability to contribute

towards

towards the public good, and becaufe even the poffible proportion of that ability does not at all keep pace with the number of men; for there is always a much greater number of citizens than of ftatefmen, or men of parts. A fingle citizen, who has faved his country, is worth a hundred thoufand others, and he ought to have as much fway as that hundred thoufand. By a fituation of legal equality, therefore, I underſtand, in gene●, that fituation in which every member of the ſtate is equally fecured from every fpecies of violence, and therefore naturally proud of his equality in point of perfonal liberty, and his fuperiority in that refpect to the fubject of a monarchical form of government.

This equality is obfervable in all free countries, where the little do not ftand in awe of the great, but both yield obedience to the laws whofe fubjects they are; where a man is not accounted a criminal, becaufe he may have incurred the anger of a grandee, and where the poor are looked upon as making part of mankind. The founders of the ancient republics thought abfolute equality fo indifpenfably neceffary, that they divided the land they poffeffed in equal fhares to every citizen: a potent meafure, but which in thefe times would be chimerical and impracticable, to augment the love and fidelity of every member of the commonwealth,

wealth, towards his country. In former times, the acquifition of too great perfonal confideration was looked upon as a crime againft the ftate; becaufe, wherever any one was exalted above the law, all others muft be dependent on him. The punifh-ment of the Oftracifm was introduced by the Athenians, folely with the view of fecuring the re-public from the predominancy of great men over the lower clafs. Proceeding on the fame principle, the Venetians once condemned one of their magif-trates to death, becaufe he had, of a fudden, ap-peafed a very dangerous fedition; for, they faid, " he who can fo eafily pacify fuch an infurrection, is able to raife one at any time." For the fame reafon, in fome modern republics, no man can with impunity be noble, wealthy, juft, or eminent for his talents. Inftead of ftriving with a competitor worthy of rivalfhip, a great man finds a competitor in every fool: and for this reafon, a peafant of the canton of Appenzel once fhrewdly remarked to my friend, the worthy Dr. Hirzell, " that the inhabitants of a certain republican city had cut off the head of one of their fellow-citizens, becaufe it was the only head among them."

In fome modern republics, the legal inequality of rank and confideration is concealed as much as poffible under the appearance of equality; the chief men treat each other as if they were all of the fame

6   rank,

rank, equally wealthy, and all upon a level with refpect to underftanding and virtue. In republics, fuperior merit, unfcreened by the reverence which in monarchies is attached to the privileged orders, is always the prey of envy, wherefore the chiefs treat the fubjects of their republic, collectively, with affability, courtefy, and love; they feem all to affect thofe beneficent virtues, which proceed from an enlightened underftanding and are the true caufe of the preference given to rule over happy and free men rather than over a herd of flaves. The Carnival was merely inftituted at Venice with a view of hiding the great inequality of conditions in that republic, for a few months in the year, under mafks of the fame kind; and even Cofmo de Medicis exercifed his power in Florence, over a people who efteemed liberty as Heaven's beft gift, without any exterior mark to diftinguifh him from the other citizens, and as he himfelf ufed to fay, in an old great coat.

The felf-efteem of a republican, which has the jufteft foundation, is that arifing from the fenfe of perfonal fecurity. This advantage is feldom found in democracies, where a ftate of uncurbed freedom is generally a feverifh paroxyfm, in which the body politic cannot long remain. This fecurity did not exift in the Grecian ftates, where every thing fubmitted to the caprice of an haughty, blind, and

paffionate

paffionate multitude, pufhing all their paffions to
excefs, and condemning in rage to-morrow, what
they approved with rapture to-day. This advantage
was, above all, wanting at Athens, where the power
of the mob was unlimited, and the authority of the
magiftrates an empty name; where the commands
of the council were eluded, and its decifions an-
nulled, when they happened not to coincide with
the opinions of an infolent populace, whofe affem-
blies were often nothing but a folemn invitation to
the perpetration of iniquity.

On the contrary, in republics of a mixed conftitution, we may with juftice look for fecurity, and
efpecially in thofe ariftocratical ftates which, by the
ftability of their laws and the fplendor of their
government, moft refemble a limited monarchy;
and which, for that very reafon, are preferable to
all other republican conftitutions. Under fuch an
adminiftration, every individual is fure of juftice;
and the fummary mode of doing one's felf right by
the ftilletto, or a pocket piftol, is folely in vogue on
the other fide the Alps, where juftice is either too
flow or too expenfive. Each preferves his own
property, and thinks himfelf happy becaufe he cul-
tivates his field for himfelf, and pays nothing for
that liberty which is elfewhere obtained, only by
fubmitting to the moft exorbitant exactions.
Lord and mafter of himfelf and his property, he

has to account to no one for his income, or his
expenditure; and is amenable to no authority
but that of the law, for what he does, or what he
neglects; and to talk of the abfolute will of one,
excites his derifion. A nobler pride, therefore,
cannot arife in the breaft of a republican, than
when he confiders the abject fituation of the fubjects of defpotifm, depending entirely on the blind
will of one.

Defpotifm in a ftate, is like malignity in bodily
difeafes; fometimes it is the chief ailment, at others,
only an adventitious fymptom. But whenever one
individual obtains the power, he generally acquires
at the fame time the will of becoming a tyrant,
for moft men are too fond of fafhioning law after
their own will. The defire of commanding over
our equals, is the reigning paffion of the human
foul; and the rage of fuperiority refides in every
heart, but moftly where it is accompanied by a
weak head. That republic, however, will foon be
enflaved by a tyrant, where men are bafe enough
to fhew a cringing fubmiffion to the opinions or
confideration of one man, whatever pre-eminent
advantages he may enjoy above the reft of the
community. There are inftances of this in many
petty cities, pretending to be free, in which the
whole little body of the ftate, notwithftanding their
boafted independence, follow, like a flock of fheep,

the

the opinions and will of one alone ; and where this fort of tyranny is looked upon as a family right, nay an inheritance, which may pafs down unimpaired even in the female line : But we need not be very quick-fighted, to perceive what actuates thofe fpirits in places of the above defcription, who are implacable and fworn enemies of all the patriots of Europe; and who maintain, with brazen foreheads, that whoever ftands up in favour even of conftitutional liberty in a free country is literally a rebel.

But I do not mean, at prefent, to treat of any other kind of defpotifm, than that furrounded by guards, which fits on the thrones of kings, on the feats of princes, or, at leaft, in their neighbourhood; under whofe iron fceptre, all who unfortunately live within its reach, muft bow, and whofe principles and actions they are forced to approve, however repugnant or inimical to the happinefs, or even to the exiftence of a whole nation.

In fuch countries, it is the tyrant alone who is allowed to have a will ; and he does all he wills, even while he wills nought but what injures the rights of man. Whatever he covets, muft be conformable to divine and human laws ; and he but feldom defires what is not prohibited. Cambyfes, the fucceffor of Cyrus, wifhed to marry his own fifter, and inquired of his fages, whether there was no law by which fuch a marriage could be allowed ? Thefe lawyers, not lefs ingenious and fubtile than thofe of modern times, replied, " There is no law that permits the marriage of a brother with his fifter, but there is one that fays, whatever a king thinks fhall be law."

This is the fole rule of defpots; as well of him who fits on a throne, as of him who fills the inter- mediate fpace between the monarch and the fubject; or even of thofe tyrants in miniature, a defpotic no- bility, poffeffing power of life and death over the pea- fantry attached to the foil like cattle. Unacquainted with the feelings of humanity, a tyrant looks down on his fubjects as beafts of the field, fent into the world to be miferable, and to live and die under his yoke, as animals which he feeds becaufe they are adapted to hard labour ; which he has care taken of when they are fick, becaufe they are ufeful when in health ; which he fattens, that he may confume their fat ; and which he in the end flays, to make their hides ferve to harnefs others under the fame yoke.

It is in confequence of this, that the fubjects of a defpotic government make fo beggarly an appear- ance ; their dwellings are on this account cramped, their furniture mean, their whole appearance penu- rious and fqualid, and both themfelves and their

cattle

cattle the living images of famine; not even a dog
is to be found in tolerable plight; the gardens, the
groves, the bufhes are deftitute of their feathered
fongfters; all is folitary and forlorn; the poor
birds fly far away to happier climes, to avoid the
eager purfuit of the half-ftarved peafants, whom
ftern neceffity often renders expert fowlers. The
fields lie uninclofed, and are tilled with reluctance
and forrow. No cheering profpect of meadows or
of cultivated fields relieve the eye; no barns, no cow-
houfes, no hillocks of rich manuring dung, no horfes
for the plough, which, on the contrary, is dragged
o'er the half-furrowed fields by a lean afs, a lame
cow, and an old goat, yoked together; and to
complete the picture of mifery, behold in the back
ground, the hufbandman either driven to defpair and
fuicide, or to rage and murder, by the oppreffion
and cruelty of this arbitrary government.

How fhall the prince, repofing in the lap of
luxury and eafe, perceive the diftreffes, the wants,
and the univerfal defpondency of his famifhed and
defolate provinces? He acquires his revenue with
tranquillity and compofure, as long as any thing is
offered. Every thing that furrounds him confpires to
fhut his eyes and ears to the tears and groans of his
people; and the moft reafonable complaints urged
againft his counfellors are punifhed as offences
againft majefty itfelf. His agents do not ceafe tell-
ing

ing him, he may and can do whatever he pleafes, in order that he may allow them to do what they pleafe; they continually affure him his people are happy, even at the moment they are bufy in fqueezing the laft drop of fweat and blood out of them : and if they fometimes take the ability of the nation into confideration, their view is only to calculate how many moments it can live under their gripe, without entirely giving up the ghoft.

The above is a true picture of Morocco, fince the Cheriffs have brought it under their yoke; the religion, the laws, the ancient cuftoms, the prejudices imbibed by the Moors, all contribute to render the power of the monarch abfolute and unlimited ; and the fubjects, a defpicable herd, a flock of timorous fheep, without activity or will.   His power extends not only over their lives and property, but likewife over their confciences; of which, as reprefentative of their holy prophet Mahomet, he is the fpiritual director.   The people are educated from their infancy in the notion, that to die by the command of the emperor, confers an undoubted right to the joys of Paradife; and the honour to be difpatched by the emperor's own hand, a diploma for a more exalted degree of beatitude.   This explains the otherwife unaccountable inftances we fee in Morocco of cruelty, oppreffion, and tyranny on one fide; and of flavery, fubmiffion, and mifery

on the other.   The emperor is both legiſlator and
judge, and, when he is in the humour, the execu-
tioner too, of his people ; the ſole heir of their
poſſeſſions, of which he grants to the neareſt relations as much as he thinks fit.   Yet he allows a
ſhadow of authority, in matters of religion, to the
Mufti ; and he gracioufly permits his meaneſt ſubject to inſtitute a ſuit at law againſt himſelf, in
which the plaintiff is not only ſure to be nonſuited,
but alſo to be involved in the moſt unavoidable
perdition.

Muley Iſmael, emperor of Morocco, killed with
his own hand, during the time he reigned, forty
thouſand of his ſubjects : yet he was in a very
particular manner attached to juſtice.   One of his
officers complained to him that his wife, when in
ill-humour, had a cuſtom of pulling him by his
beard ; and the emperor was ſo provoked at the
impudence of this woman, that, in order to prevent
her from again offending the majeſty of his officer's
countenance, he cauſed the hairs of his beard to be
plucked out, one by one, by the roots.   He once
ſaw another of his officers on the road, driving a
flock of ſheep before him : " Whoſe ſheep are
theſe ?" interrogated the emperor ; the officer replied with the deepeſt reverence, " O Iſmael,
ſon of Elcheriff, of the ſeed of Haſſan, they are
mine."   " Thine, villain ?" ſaid the ſervant of the
Lord,

Lord, as the emperor is ftyled, " thine? I thought
I was the only proprietor in my dominions :" and
immediately, thrufting his lance through the heart
of the unfortunate fheep-driver, divided his flock
among his guards.   The only good deed that ·
Muley Ifmael feems to have done in his life, was
the deliverance of his empire from numerous bands
of robbers ; but even this only good action bore the
ftamp of his fanguinary character.   He ordered the
maffacre of all the inhabitants, men, women, and
children, of a wide extent of country, round every·
place where a robbery had been committed.   When
he gave audience to foreign minifters, he was ufually
on horfeback, in an open court ; round him ftood
his feveral officers barefooted, trembling, bowed to
the ground, and, at every word he uttered, they repeated in chorus, " Great is the wifdom of our
Lord, and the voice of our Lord is as the voice
of an Angel from Heaven."   But their Lord never
difmiffed an ambaffador till he had given him ocu-
lar demonftration of his readinefs and dexterity
in murdering fome of his fubjects ; and this entertainment generally concluded the ceremonies of
audience.

   Though all tyrants, it is true, do not act exactly
like Muley Ifmael, yet they go upon the fame principle, that their will is the only law.   I fhall fpare
myfelf the chagrin of citing examples of chriftian
                                        princes,

princes, whofe pleafure feems rather to confift in procreating their fpecies, than in exterminating it ; but who, in every other inftance, are as lawlefs tranfgreffors againft humanity, but have not the candour to declare, what John Galeas Duke of Milan faid, " that he extirpated the robbers that infefted his territories, only in order to be the only one of that vocation."

But Afia is the quarter of the globe where ty- ranny is ever wakeful and ever predominant, deeply fixing the eternal principles of deftruction, under the pretence of momentary advantage ; granting but the wretched confolation of tears and lamentations to the nations it devours, that the great and their inftruments may live in plenty and fecurity, who repay with intereft, to the defencelefs people, thofe lafhes they receive from their lord. Property in land has been fet afide in Turkey, Perfia, and the Mogul empire : the governor of a province fays, " Why fhould not I be a wolf, for I am mafter of the fheep-fold ?" The countryman fays, " Where- fore fhall I labour for a tyrant, who will to-morrow plunder me of what I have to-day earned by the fweat of my brow ?"   When the Turkifh bafhaws travel, they are not content with eating the pea- fants out of houfe and home, confuming whatever is confumable ; but, when with their numerous at- tendants their bellies are well filled, they are uncon-

fcientious

fcientious enough to exact a contribution in money, which they call tooth-money, or an acknowledgment for the ufe of their teeth, which they have worn down by granting the farmer the honour of devouring his victuals. Hence the dreadful pictures travellers give us of the prefent fituation of the Afiatic ftates: hence they fay, that the formerly fo happy Mofopotamia, bleffed Paleftine, and the admired plains of Antioch, are now almoft as miferable and as barren as the modern Campania of Rome; which is naked and defolate, deftitute of inhabitants, without inclofures, without corn-fields, without a tree, without a bufh, without houfes, nay nearly without even a bramble.

The power of the emperor of China is, in that civilized and praife-worthy country, abfolute and unlimited: he reprefents a fort of deity; and the veneration fhewn towards him approaches near to adoration; his difcourfes are liftened to as oracles, and his decifions are followed as if they came immediately from the higheft Heaven. In Perfia, the commands of the king are punctually executed, although his majefty might happen to be drunk when he iffued them. In Japan, it would be thought a derogation to the imperial dignity, if the emperor was to inflict any punifhment lefs than death.

The

The viciſſitude of fortune is no where ſo great as under deſpotic governments. Perſian princes of the blood-royal were compelled to become ſchool-maſters and uſhers; and Kouli Khan left many of his miniſters no other reſource for their daily bread. The great men at court are hourly deprived of their places at Conſtantinople; and the longeſt life of thoſe who are the moſt fortunate there, is nothing but a life of uncertainty, ſuſpicion, and fear. Under the laſt dynaſty in China, princes of the imperial blood were actually ſeen in the condition of porters, and only diſtinguiſhed from others of the ſame vocation by their belts and cords being of yellow ſilk, which colour is excluſively permitted to the Imperial family.

A cane, in China, ſupplies the place of the law. The courts of juſtice of this great empire cauſe their paternal corrections, as they are called, to be adminiſtered in twenty hard blows, which people of rank muſt ſubmit to as well as the lower orders. The ſmalleſt overſight in words or geſtures is puniſhed with the baſtinado; and when the of-fender is ſufficiently cudgelled, he falls on his knees before the judge, bows his forehead thrice to the ground, and gives thanks for the care taken for his inſtruction and amendment.

The power of the emperor of China reſts, like that of all other tyrants, upon the daſtardy of his ſubjects;

fubjects ; their abjectnefs is fo great, that flavery is
not even thought difgraceful. An opulent Tartar
or Chinefe mandarin has many flaves in his fervice,
he himfelf is the flave of another greater court lord,
and this laft again the flave of the emperor. The
Chinefe in chains have loft every thing, even the
wifh of breaking them.

Defpotifm is faid to have no where been fo mild
and moderate as in the kingdom of Tanjour, on
the coaft of Coromandel. Raguola Naicher, who
occupied this throne in the laft century, was fo juft
and equitable that his memory is ftill revered; he
took but two thirds of the fruits of the earth from
his fubjects, and in the night he caufed fearch to be
made after fuch as might ftand in need of relief.

A true republican muft therefore neceffarily be
juftly proud of a government under which he enjoys liberty and fecurity, when he confiders, that in
the moral as well as the phyfical world there are
large and fmall pifmires, between whom there exifts fuch an inveterate and inborn hatred, that the
great never reft till they have exterminated the
little ones.

CHAPTER THE SIXTEENTH.

OF PRIDE IN MONARCHIES.

I HAVE fomewhere read, that men are feldom fit to govern themfelves, and that their vanity fubmits with lefs reluctance to the dominion of one, than the equality of many.

Thefe are not the opinions entertained in republics on this head; but in this Chapter I fhall depart a good deal from my own ideas, and offer in lieu of them, the obfervations and opinions of fubjects of monarchical ftates, in order to explain more clearly how that form of government can elevate the heart.

By pride in monarchical ftates, I underftand, the elevation of mind felt by a whole nation, when it finds itfelf peculiarly happy in the perfon of its fovereign; the power of doing good without limitation, the power of doing evil without the will, promifes a golden age to the people as long as the will of the monarch is directed by great and good views.

views. The glory of that empire, which in Europe
moſt looks up to its king, will always be ſuperior to
that of any other empire on earth, as long as its
king is what he ought to be.

The ſubjects of a monarchy are, in our times, by
no means all abject creatures, unleſs by their abſurd
cowardice they make themſelves ſo. We now ſee
benevolent monarchs filling European thrones,
friends to the pacific virtues, to the arts and ſciences ; fathers of their people, crowned citizens ;
and miniſters at their ſides, who equally deſerve a
crown. The ancients had no idea of the temperate
ſyſtem of our monarchies ; their governments were
either entirely republican, or entirely deſpotic.
They did not know that the time would come
when thoſe barbarous ages would be no more,
when a tyrant aſſumed an abſolute control over
our thoughts and actions ; and that the ſubject of
a monarchy could be as much a citizen, as the
citizen of the freeſt republican ſtate is a ſubject.
They did not know that the time would come
when the ſame might be ſaid of limited monarchies,
which they boaſted of in their republics, that not
man but law was the ſovereign. They did not
know that order, ſyſtem, and perſeverance could
exiſt under the ſhade of monarchical power ; that
property might be ſecured, and that we may ſit-
down in the circle of our duties at eaſe, and duly
                                        attend

attend to them; while all the arts flourish around us, every thing excites to emulation, and the fovereign may live in the midst of his people like a father among his children.

It is a difcovery of the prefent age, that a certain fpirit of freedom can exift under a kingly government. The fpirit of liberty of a Montefquieu, a d'Alembert, an Helvetius, a Mably, a Chalotais, a Thomas, a Marmontel, and fo many other Frenchmen of the firft rank in literature, is the greateft fatire on the notion entertained by fome refpecting republics; and it tends to prove that monarchy produces fometimes as great effects, and contributes as much to univerfal felicity as republicanifm itfelf. All depends immediately upon the king in perfon, or upon his prime minifter. We always fee that their manners have as much influence on liberty as the laws; that they can turn men into beafts, and beafts into men; that they will have fubjects when they love free fouls, and flaves when they prefer bafe and fordid minds. The Duke of Choifeul's name and memory will be cherifhed by the lateft pofterity; for he has required fome of the beft heads in France to examine the principles of his adminiftration, and to judge of its effects on the happinefs or mifery of that great kingdom; and he has promifed to avail himfelf of the lights they may furnifh him for the improvement or alteration of his

P   fyftem.

fyftem. This franknefs, fo nobly courted in an entire monarchical government, would in many a
republic be thought a crime againft the ftate; while,
on the contrary, it has already produced fuch edicts
at Verfailles as muft greatly conduce to the augment-
ation of the power and confideration of France;
if this fyftem can be perfevered in, and the attacks
of felf-intereft, the moft inimical motive that can
exift to this kind of improvement, can be parried
with fkill and firmnefs.

All the faculties of the mind and of the heart
rife into action under a wife monarch. In republics,
a phlegmatic indifferent man is a good citizen, and
fuch are held the beft for the intereft of the ftate:
a man, whofe talents are fuperior to thofe of the
multitude, is dangerous; he would be a better citizen
if he were more a fool; his actions and motives are
narrowly pried into by fufpicion as well as jealoufy,
and the nobleft mind, therefore, often fhrouds itfelf in
obfcurity and lives in a painful inactivity. But under
the aufpices of an intelligent monarch, a wide field
is opened for the exercife of the powers of the mind;
where talents run the race of emulation, and merit
obtains the prize; where the character is ftamped
with greatnefs; where genius unfolds itfelf; where
wifdom and virtue break through the croud, and
dare advance with unabafhed countenances. Where
virtue is honoured, there it refides. Riches are
defpifed,

defpifed; when compared to the moft infignificant trifles which are beftowed as pledges of the gratitude and efteem of an enlightened monarch. He is the magnet which attracts the greateft talents and moft elevated virtues, the hand that fafhions them; the breath that animates them, and the centre of their activity. The moft comprehenfive faculties lie motionlefs and becalmed, if not called into action by the fovereign.

A monarch does not fhine forth a confpicuous object to pofterity, elevated as it were upon the fhoulders of his people, if he leaves them undiftinguifhed beneath him. They together afcend to the fame height; with the only difference, that the prince ftands at the head of a happy people, and the greatnefs of his name is written on every forehead. The glory of the monarch extends over his nation, and all thofe great men who, by their deferts participate in this glory, though they glitter likewife for themfelves, yet their luftre is alfo reflected on the enlightened monarch who knew how to employ their talents. A king, therefore, who underftands the true art of government, concentrates the whole worth of his nation in himfelf, and his glory is infeparable from that of his people.

It has been obferved, that the art of governing with honour requires but one talent, and but one virtue, refpectively dependant on each other; this

virtue

virtue is that of philanthropy, and the proper application of it is the talent required. When a king
is ſeriouſly and heartily inclined to do good, and
employs with ſcrupulous diſcernment the moſt infallible means in his power to accompliſh this glorious purpoſe, the honour that ariſes to him from
his efforts only returns to its own ſource. A king,
who unites every part of his territories by the bands
of confidence and love into one body, of which he
is the ſoul, who encourages population and induſ-
try, who promotes agriculture and trade, who
awakens and rewards the arts, who calls talents
into action and gives protection to virtue: ſuch a
king accumulates in the lap of peace an immenſe
treaſure of glory, without its coſting his ſubjects
a ſingle tear or the world one drop of blood;
an harveſt which is reaped by the hand which
ſowed it, and enjoyed by thoſe who aſſiſt in collect-
ing it.

This ever-exiſting intimate connection between
the glory of a monarch and that of his ſubjects, is
the chief foundation of noble pride in monarchical
ſtates; every ſubject appropriates to himſelf a part
of the glory of his ſovereign, and in the ſame manner, the ſovereign is irradiated by that which his
ſubjects acquire.

The ſpirit of rapine in a monarch cannot, it is
true, induce any one of his ſubjects, who is in his

right

right fenfes, to boaft of it. The man who is in the fervice of his king and his country, may carry arms in a good or in a bad caufe; he may have received the fword from the hand of juftice or from that of ambition; he cares not why or wherefore; he is neither looked to as the author, the juftifier, or the guarantee of the plan he carries into execution; his perfonal honour is fecured to him, and he is the more refpected in proportion to the energy with which he executes his duty. - An extraordinary ftrength of mind, and talents of the firft rate, may make him feel the mifery which they occafion in the world, and may fupprefs the emotions of pride; but when the genius of war animates a royal breaft, and far fuperior to the furprizing difclofure of natural powers, far fuperior to the effects of a fpirit of contention, it is founded on juftice, then every feeling mind exalts itfelf with the king, and is juftly proud of a monarch who, broiling in the mid-day fun, and covered with duft and blood, performs wonders at the head of his fubjects.

Of fuch a king, his fubjects will with juftice be proud; who has paffed the days of his youth in folitude; who has fhook hands with misfortune, in the years of pleafure; and in the feafon of tranquil enjoyment has learned to be a king, a philofopher, a legiflator, a hero, and a man.

Under

Under fuch a king, the genius of a nation will take a new flight; the arts and fciences will rife into juft eftimation; philofophy will no more be pedantry; and even courtiers will become philofophers, when the king defpifes that frivoloufnefs which, among the great, conftitutes what they call high life; and which is excufable in thofe fhallow harmlefs kings, who, feated on the throne, are tired with doing nothing. Liberty of opinion will prefent an undaunted front; perfecuted virtue will find an afylum; and oppreffed innocence, a fhield: the fpirit of perfecution will recoil through its own fubterraneous paffages to the dungeons of defpair, and the injured will be revenged, when, by an ineftimable piece of good fortune, philofophy, united to fovereign power, affifts in chafing from the throne thofe vices which are deftructive of the rights of man. Every path to fame will be open to the people, when the monarch treads each path before them; and no nobler incentive to literary exertions can exift, than when the royal pen flows with genius and wit; when the hiftory it traces is truth, and the poetry it produces is pregnant with thought and fpirit. Favourites will become fincere, and politicians honeft, if he tears the mafk of flattery from the face of falfehood, and that of policy from cunning. Innocence will never murmur againft its judges, and juftice and equity will ceafe bleeding at every pore, if the monarch fhews his indignation

againft

againſt the ſpirit of litigation, and forces it back to the hell it came from; leaving its encouragers and protectors, the lawyers and their dependants, to get their bread by honeſt means or ſtarve.

The ſubjects of ſuch a king will cheriſh the moſt juſtifiable pride, when he extends his regard as well to the humbleſt among them as to his choiceſt friends; when he adopts every meaſure requiſite to enſure the meaneſt peaſant as much real happineſs as the higheſt peer; when his preſence fills the court with the awe of majeſty, and the cottage of the labourer with chearfulneſs and content.

The ſoul of ſuch a monarch will animate his army; when in war, he ſhares with his ſoldiers the fatigues of a march, the inclemencies of the ſeaſon, and the want of all conveniencies, and often of the neceſſaries of life; when he ſmiles with complacency on their bands as they paſs in review before him; when he mixes in the middle of them, cordially preſſes their rough hands, and inſpires their ſouls with the ſame heroic hilarity he himſelf feels at the ſight of them; when he goes into their tents and converſes with eaſe and familiarity, gaily with the merry, tenderly with the unhappy; enquiring with ſympathy after their wounds, and ſharing the ſmart of them; ſtriving to conquer the impatience of ſuffering, and ſupporting the heroiſm of their ſouls

even

even in death; when within fight of the enemy, by a penetrating and quick glance of all that is neceffary to the fuccefs of a comprehenfive and well combined plan, he regulates the prefent by his experience of the paft; always can feize the fleeting, the decifive moment of advantage, and preffing forward at the head of his troops, carrying the banner of death before him, in the very heat of the battle, furrounded by innumerable and imminent dangers, and fighting in the thickeft throngs of the enemy, can with an unfhaken prefence of mind, obferve at one glance both danger and deliverance.

The fubjects of fuch a king will with joy, in the middle of numerous and impending perils, look forward to the day on which his glory will be firmly eftablifhed; when they behold the moft powerful and warlike nations, and who are the beft appointed to ftrive for the empire of the world, rife up againft him; their country attacked on all fides, nearly over-run by its enemies, and fhaken to its very foundations; their monarch, long unacquainted with reft and eafe, in order to procure thefe comforts to his fubjects, watching many a tedious night, while protected and fecured by his plans and precautions, they lie in foft and undifturbed repofe; when they fee him, ever more fudden than danger, more vigilant than artifice, impetuous and irrefiftible as the whirlwind of heaven, flying with his fuc-

cour

cour from one province to another, and delivering
innocence from deſtruction and rapine, wherever
they appear ; when, by his unheard-of exploits, he
extorts admiration as well from his noble-minded
enemies as from his moſt zealous friends, and attracts the eyes of the whole world ; when he is
quick, vigorous, eager, and impreſſive, often making
powerful and deciſive exertions, ſometimes ſtriking
ſhort of his aim, ſometimes receiving injury from the
recoil of his blow ; not following circumſtances, but
bending them to his purpoſe; not removing obſtacles,
but over-leaping them; and ever greateſt where he has
to redreſs a fault ; when, vanquiſhed, ſometimes by
nature, ſometimes by numbers, ſometimes by heroes
he has formed and taught to conquer, he ever knows
how to pluck deliverance from danger, and redemp-
tion from the brink of a precipice; when every miſ-
fortune is but the never failing forerunner of a great
and ſurpriſing effort of courage and prudence; when
his loſſes lead him to new victories, and reſembling
nothing but himſelf, great and unexampled both in
proſperity and calamity, he now triumphs over his
enemies, and now over his misfortunes.

Every patriotic ſoul will more than ever glow for
him, when, over the widely extended graves of the
victors and the vanquiſhed, the wearied world ſhall re-
echo with the joyful ſound of peace, and the monarch,
greater even than in war, ſhall, on the feſtive day of

his

his return to his royal city, steal away from the loud acclamations and heart-felt exultations and bleffings of the multitude, to vifit in folitude a neighbouring field of battle, and calling the adjacent peafantry around him, shall enquire with folicitude and earneftnefs after their prefent fituation, the number of cattle they now have, and the loffes they have fuftained by the operations of war; and alleviating, by every means in his power, the diftreffes they have undergone, shall at night, difdaining the offenfive pomp of a triumphal entry, return to his palace by an unfrequented and unfufpected paffage.

The nobleft pride can thus exift in monarchies, when the fovereign and his adminiftration are what they ought to be.

CHAPTER THE SEVENTEENTH.

REFLECTIONS ON SOME ADVANTAGES AND DISADVANTAGES OF NATIONAL PRIDE, AS FOUNDED UPON REAL EXCELLENCIES.

I AM aware that many pointed, farcaftical remarks, occurring in this treatife, will have called down upon my head the bittereft execrations of wounded pride, which will have invoked heaven and earth, fire and water, hell and the devil, and all their concomitants and dependants, to revenge its ideal wrong; and I muft ftill humbly folicit my pardon, for the wholefome but galling truths which may now and then be found in this my laft chapter.

An elevation of heart, repofing on a real and folid foundation, is certainly of great utility in fome cafes, and is even fanctioned and approved of by religion. Although we cannot boaft of our merits before God, yet religion infpiring us with the fenfe of the greatnefs of our deftination, and the means by which it may be attained, exalts our whole foul; while Divine Providence and mercy infufe into us a

fteady

steady confidence and renovated powers, to appreciate and depend upon our own exertions, never
leaving us to sink under the weaknesses of human
nature.   Humility of heart can very well exist with
perseverance, resolution, elevation of soul, and, in
general, with every consequence of a cheerful consciousness of our good qualities and perfections;
provided we never lose sight of our dependance on
God, and the consideration that he is the mediate
or immediate source of every good.   A certain degree of self-satisfaction too often, indeed, appears
through the veil of humility; but real humility
does not require of us to deny the good we really
possess, or to prize it at a lower rate than it in
fact deserves; so that religion, far from condemning a noble elevation of heart, is rather a stable
foundation for it, since it does not require the knowledge of ourselves, only for the purpose of subdu-
ing our vain-glory, but for that of making us sensible of the faculties and advantages we have received
from the Creator, and exciting us to employ them
in a manner suitable to his glory and our own happiness.

A confidence in these faculties and advantages,
and the firm belief in eternal truth and justice
arising therefrom, produces a strength and con-
stancy of soul which repels the ruling abuses and
prejudices of a country; a courage to withstand an
universal

univerfal hatred, and out of refpect for truth, to fet at nought the opinions of the many.

This confidence in one's own refources begets that afpiring fentiment of fuperiority, without which a man cannot attempt any noble deed; deprived of this confidence, the braveft man finks into a ftate of dulnefs and inactivity, by which his foul is fettered and debafed as in a narrow prifon, where it fhould feem to be endowed with power only to endure, where the heavy load of calamity wholly preffes down the heart, where every duty is a burden, the leaft labour dreaded, and every future profpect gloomy and cheerlefs. Every path to fame and honour is inacceffible to him, and his fpirit lies motionlefs and dejected, like the hardy polar navigator, who finds himfelf hemmed in and furrounded on every fide by a vaft continent of ice. He arrives at nothing, for he afpires to nothing; and he afpires not, becaufe he is diffident of his faculties. For this reafon, we often fee people of much lower merit, the foremoft in the road to fortune, only becaufe their character is more enterprifing and undaunted.

It is from this fame degrading and too low opinion of ourfelves, that one man becomes the flave of another. I fee, with heartfelt forrow, men of merit fall into the extremeft felf-contempt, with regard to great men, on whom, perhaps, fometimes their fortune

tune depends; but who do not even require this abafement. '

   'I have often heard a language held which is called humility; but is in fact, abjectnefs of mind; which, for the fake of a livelihood hardly earned, or for an ill-requited fervice, fets a great man in the place of a deity; and would only be worthy of an Algerine flave; crouching before his Dey. Such language penetrates my very foul, as it debafes human nature itfelf; befides, more true refpect is ever fhewn to greatnefs, when we fpeak our fentiments freely and nobly. Whoever falls into the fault; either in reality or in appearance, to efteem himfelf lefs than he ought to do; becomes the flave of every one who chufes to make him fo. The fear of lofing his daily bread deprives his foul of all its energy, fwells every guinea to a mountain's fize, and ftamps every expreffion with the character of the moft cringing fervitude, unlefs a man be unconquerably attached to his native liberty. With thofe who are fo miferably dependant on the fmiles of the great for temporary fuftenance, the opinion of their own meannefs fwallows up all ideas of the innate dignity of human nature, of nobility of fentiment, of felf-confidence, and of their competence to judge for themfelves concerning what is right or wrong; they, at laft, in reality, turn the heads of thofe otherwife good-natured nobles, by ever crouching before
them

them as before the throne of a tyrant, and by looking up to them with the fame fearful and forrowful countenance as a friar does to his abbot under
whose tremendous cenfure he has fallen. . . . .
. . . .

From this fame too humiliating opinion of themfelves, men become the flaves, of their paffions
and unfaithful to the purpofes of their creation.
More confidence in their own powers would prove
to them, that it is poffible to be virtuous amidft
temptation, and that they may rife from the fafcina-
ting couch of luxury and pleafure triumphant over
both. Were the Afcetics endowed with this confidence, they need not ufe fuch exertions to deftroy
the match at which love takes fire. . . . .

We become unfaithful to the purpofes of our
creation when we do not poffefs thofe folid principles which hardens us againft fuffering. Every
man of underftanding is of no ufe to fociety, if,
in a joylefs retirement of the world, he has not
learned to bear with all that can wound the finer
fentiments, diffipate or oppofe the foftnefs of humanity, and pierce the tendernefs of heart arifing
from it. He ceafes to exert his faculties, when he
daily fees people around him, who do not know
that their underftanding and tafte may be improved
and fharpened, by a thoufand things whofe names
they are even ignorant of; and, who of courfe
heartily

heartily hate the commanding influence of under-ftanding and tafte. He fnatches at momentary joys, and unnerves all the powers of his foul, to be admitted into their fociety. He oppofes the opinions of no man, let them be ever fo abfurd. He pretends not to correct any prejudice or error, determined, as Triftram Shandy very juftly fays to his mule, " never to argue a point with any one of that family as long as he lives."

Except within the ever-cheering bounds of religion, it is impoffible to find a more powerful fupport under misfortune than in a reafonable felf-efteem. Let a worthy man, when perfecuted and difgraced, only afk himfelf, who are they who are always planning my deftruction, who openly defpife me, abufe, calumniate, and fcoff at me? Are they not, to a man, fools and blockheads? and fuch people can be as little friends to enlightened minds, as thieves are to honefty: hence it is an honour to be an object of their abufe. Every man of fenfe fhould adhere to thefe fentiments; he fhould be confcious that he is above meddling with this infect tribe. But if he has repelled their attacks, and fees that flander now only dares whifper its malice, and dart its venom behind his back, he will fmile at its vain efforts, and think thefe people are heavily loaden with fpite, and muft difcharge it at all events, or fink under it.

A re-

A reliance on good fortune, or that extraordinary concurrence of events we do not forefee, fupports a man in imminent danger, elevates his foul, and leffens that dread which he otherwife would feel in his mind, when about to execute fome great achieve- ment, he fees and weighs the difficulties and dangers he has to encounter. This reliance on his good fortune produced that noble prefumption which Cæfar, when yet but young, fhewed during his imprifonment in the ifland of Pharmacufa among the pirates of Cilicia; who were then, by reafon of their large fhips and numerous fleets, mafters of the fea, and, at the fame time, men of the moft fanguinary character. Cæfar fent all his attendants to the adjacent towns to collect money for his ranfom, and ftayed, accompanied only by his phyfician and two fervants, with thefe barbarians, whom he treated with great contempt; often, when he went to reft, he ordered them to be filent, and not to difturb his fleep. The Cilicians required twenty talents for his ranfom, and Cæfar laughing at them, as if they did not know what a valuable prifoner they had, promifed them fifty: he con- tinued perfectly eafy and intrepid for near fix weeks, jefting and diverting himfelf with thefe rude outlaws; he compofed difcourfes and poems, which he read to them, and called fuch as were not affected by them barbarians and ideots: he went fo far, as often to affure them, with a laugh-

Q.

ing countenance, that he would have them all hanged; and, in fact, he had hardly regained his freedom, before, taking some ships which he found in the harbour of Melitum, he directly attacked these pirates close to Pharmacusa, took the greatest part of them prisoners, and condemned them to be crucified. This same reliance on his good fortune caused in this same Cæsar the memorable instance of intrepidity he shewed a few days before the battle of Pharsalia; when, disguised in the habit of a slave, he went in a little bark to meet the fleet of Anthony, which was not come up : a violent tempest arose, and threatened immediately to overwhelm them in the waves, when Cæsar, taking the trembling and desponding pilot by the hand, said, " Courage man ! you carry Cæsar and his fortunes." Columbus conjectured that a new world might be discovered, and persevering in his good fortune, he discovered America.

One man thinks himself born to misfortune, another to happiness; just as a gamester plays very badly the remainder of an evening, because he had begun by playing unluckily: the first, always deterred by fear and irresolution, never risks any thing, and will, therefore, certainly always remain in poverty, and at the same time his irresolution will make him an object of contempt and pity to others. The latter is fortunate, because he ventures as

2   much

much as may be without temerity, and a bright
day-break ·of good fortune immediately kindles in
his breaft a higher degree of hope, which we call
confidence, and procures him the efteem and refpect of others. Confidence in one's felf produces the power even of refifting time; an emulation of one's felf, to furpafs, by new deeds, our
former ones, and to eclipfe, by greater merits, thofe
which are already acknowledged to belong to us;
perfevering in our career of fortune, till we over-
take the fickle goddefs. But the greateft minds
are thofe who, convinced of the viciffitude of
human affairs, are never over-bearing in profperity,
nor caft down in adverfity.

Hence it appears, that a noble felf-efteem actually
gives us the power to exalt ourfelves above ·the
weaknefs of human nature, to exert our talents in
praife-worthy enterprifes, never to yield to the
fpirit of flavery, never to be flaves of vice, to· obey
the dictates of our confcience, to fmile under mif-
fortune, and to rely upon feeing better days.

It is of infinite confequence that this exaltation
of human nature, this confidence· in our powers,
fhould be imprinted in the bofom in the earlieft
period of life. Young minds muft be animated
with the love of what is good, noble, and great:
virtue muft be depicted to them in ftriking ex-

amples

amples to make them love virtue; we muſt inſpire them with a high opinion of their faculties, that they may venture to become virtuous and good; always teach them by repreſentation, impreſs them with the value of great deeds, by ſpeaking pictures, and encourage them to imitate what they ſee exhibited by ſenſible objects. Lavater's national ſongs, and Solomon Hirzel's hiſtorical views of the Swiſs confederacy, are put into the hands of our Helvetian youth; theſe preſent them with a picture of thoſe times, when noblenefs of ſoul was prized above every thing; when virtuous manners found univerſal eſteem, and heroic virtues, univerſal renown. In youth, we are capable of catching that bright flame which glowed in the heroes of former times, and of indulging the noble wiſh of gathering laurels in the very places where our worthy anceſtors reaped a glorious harveſt of them. The repreſentation of noble achievements, and the hiſtory of virtuous actions, have an electrical effect upon the pliant ſtem of youth; they inſpire the ſoul with admiration, and render the young men emulous of theſe examples.

Great hiſtorical events, expreſſively delineated and conveyed to the heart in glowing colours, the lives of famous men, ſuch as thoſe by Plutarch, and Caſper Hirzel, and the Poems of Geſner, imprinted with the noble and indelible marks of

nature,

nature, have, therefore, aftonifhing effects on the minds of youth. I heard my fon once, in his fifth year, afk his mother, who preffed him to her maternal bofom, while fhe explained to him Plutarch's lives, "Will my life, too, be written?" Every child, nobly born, however poor his parents may be, will defire to be great; when his heart is completely touched with the genius or virtues of great men, the fame virtues will germinate in his young mind, and he will burn with impatience to fill, with regard to pofterity, the fame poft of honour which thofe eminent men have filled before him with fuch diftinguifhed fplendour. This defire of emulation will frequently burft into tears, which every father ought to reward by the fondeft embraces.

Themiftocles was very young when the Greeks vanquifhed the Perfians at Marathon, and hearing Miltiades, to whom they owed that victory continually extolled, he became quite filent and penfive, and avoided all juvenile diverfions; his friends afked him the reafon of this change, and this noble youth anfwered, " the trophies of Miltiades will not let me fleep." Thucydides, the hiftorian, burft into tears when he heard, in his early youth, Herodotus publicly read his hiftory amidft the univerfal applaufe of all Greece in the city of Olympia. Zeno exhorted thofe who looked upon the ferious and contemplative countenance of Pericles, as a

Q 3

preof

proof of his infufferable arrogance, to be animated with the fame pride, in order to be inflamed with the fame love of the great and good, and that they might be infenfibly accuftomed to the imitation of his virtues. Demofthenes was, when a boy, fo ftruck with the renown which Calliftrates acquired by pleading, that, captivated by the fublime power of eloquence, he immediately embraced the principles of Zeno, and retired into folitude, abandoning every other ftudy for that of rhetoric, to which he entirely devoted himfelf. Homer was the author of much heroifm among the Greeks, as well as the father of poetry; it is well known how eagerly Alexander read his fublime productions. When Cæfar was reading the hiftory of that conqueror, during his refidence in Spain, he fhed tears, becaufe Alexander was at the fame age fo great, and Cæfar yet fo infignificant; not indeed, virtuous tears, but thofe of ambition, which was the ruling paffion of this future deftroyer of Roman liberty; as plainly appeared, when in paffing through a paltry infignificant village, he faid, " I would rather be the firft man here, than the fecond in Rome."

Thefe impreffions on the minds of youth, conftantly repeated, ftrengthen the foul, multiply its fprings, make every thing feem attainable to them, and ftrongly excite that noble defire of fame which always is productive of great actions when it is accompanied

companied by virtue; while, on the other hand, an utter infenfibility towards the inftances of noblenefs of foul or fuperior merit, which we meet with in hiftory, is the fureft prefage that the youth on whom they make no impreffion, will never be capable of any thing great. The Spartans underftood perfectly how to raife in their children this noble thirft of honour; a reproach was the moft poignant punifhment they could inflict; and a commendation was a rapturous reward; whoever fhewed himfelf indifferent and unmoved by either the one or the other, was defpifed at Sparta as a mean, little mind, unadapted to the exercife of any virtue. It is on this principle that, very lately, a French minifter of ftate, the Duke of Choifeul, has commanded a man of learning, who poffeffes the feelings of a citizen and the penetration of a ftatefman, to make a collection of the fine fayings and actions of French officers and foldiers, for the ufe of the military fchool at Paris; and certainly this will be the beft book that can be put into the hands of a young French foldier.

All thefe reflections, taken collectively, lead to the conclufion of the great confequence to a nation, of a noble felf-efteem, and of the important advantage refulting from it, owing to the clofe connection between a proper national pride, and the love of one's country.

When

When the example of one fingle man, taken out of a whole feries of hiftorical relations, is fuf-ficient to animate our hearts with fuch noble fenti-ments, how much more muft the accumulated ex amples of whole nations work upon our minds? Great actions, in war or in the internal government of a commonwealth, fill our bofoms with admira-tion of them and of our country, penetrating us with the inmoft veneration for thofe men who were fenfible of the pleafure of dying for their country; who did not withdraw from ferving it, though their expectations were defeated, though their difguft was ever fo much awakened, their feelings hurt, and their whole lives embittered by the fharpeft ftings of envy and malice, which they magnanimoufly bore for the honour of virtue and of their country's rights. It is for fuch men, that the reverence of a nation muft be excited, in order to beget in it a due refpect for itfelf, which alone is able to render it celebrated.

The pride arifing from the merits of fuch men gives a nation a juft claim to immortality, when thefe great examples defcending to pofterity, un-adulterated by tradition, are admired and emulated. Hence came that great and noble energy of foul and thought, with which the whole nation was animated, both among the Grecians and the Ro-mans. The love of their country was interwoven

in

in their religion, in their conſtitution, and in their manners; "Their Country" was the foul of ſociety, the univerſal topic of converſation, the word of battle, the ſound to rally by, the ſhout of victory in their bloody wars; it was the muſic that charmed them in private life, the ſinew of their actions; it inflamed their poets, their orators, and their ſenators; it reſounded from the ſtage, in the forum, in all their public aſſemblies; it was brought home to the inmoſt ſouls of their poſterity, by the public monuments erected to its honour. But in modern times, we often ſee whole nations devoid of this vivifying ſentiment; the love of their country has been transferred to the inhabitants of more than one monarchy, and in more than one republic it ſeems to be conſidered as an improper prejudice.

- While whole nations placed their honour in liberty, and this in nothing but a noble manner of thinking, the love of their country was the deareſt ſentiment of their ſouls. Stronger than ſelf-love, full of ſoftneſs, lovelineſs, and harmony; the love of their country included all that could touch the heart and elevate the ſoul; it deprived death of its ſting, and luxury of its votaries: the generous flame burned in every boſom, every heart glowed for its country. Hardened to ſuffering, inſenſible to their own inconvenience, and proportionably more zealous for the happineſs of all, they were deſirous of
nothing

nothing but what might tend to ferve their country; preferring even its honour to that of their own individual progenitors and the general good to private advantage; they thought themfelves fufficiently happy and honoured, if the republic was happy and honoured. They laid afide their private animofities and jealoufies, and laboured to promote the glory and intereft of their greateft competitors, when the public good feemed to require it. If injured by their country, they readily forgot its poignant ingratitude, and ferved it even while fmarting under its fting; they fubmitted to its caprices, as a dutiful child fubmits to the fplenetic humour of its parent. Under every kind of hardfhip they remained fteadily and warmly attached to their country, and endeavoured to conceal their own fufferings from themfelves, by fixing all their attention upon the public welfare. They broke afunder, before the altar of their country, the bands of affection, love, and tendernefs, towards parents, children, wives, and relations; they tore themfelves away from every thing that could keep them back in effeminate indolence; they were deaf to the voice of relationfhip and love, and only liftened to that of their country; they heard in the moft fearful founds of war and arms, nothing but the thanks of their country on their return; they never enquired after the number of their enemies, but where they were. Each advanced with intrepidity to the poft of

honour,

honour, which perhaps had been the grave of his gallant anceſtors at ſome former period; each preſſed forward to aſſiſt in forming a rampart for their defencelefs fellow citizens, contented if, by his fall, he could give occaſion to another to advance to the ſame glorious death on the ſame ſpot; for, it was not the ſlain who were lamented, but thoſe who ingloriouſly ſurvived.

Hipperides, the orator, bit his own tongue off when on the rack, in order to prevent the greatneſs of the torture, in which he died, from forcing him to betray his country to Antipater.

Pedaretes had not the good fortune to be choſen among the three hundred men who enjoyed in Sparta a diſtinguiſhed rank: and he went home perfeſtly contented, ſaying, " I am uncommonly happy that Sparta poſſeſſes three hundred men of greater merit than myſelf."

Before the battle of Marathon, the Athenians eleſted ten generals, who were inveſted, each in his turn, with the ſupreme command. The day approaching when it belonged to Ariſtides to aſſume it, he generouſly yielded his authority to the approved valour and experience of Miltiades. The other generals followed the illuſtrious example, ſacrificing the diſtates of private ambition to the

intereſt

intereſt and glory of their country; and the commander in chief thus enjoyed an opportunity of exerting, uncontrolled, the utmoſt vigour of his genius.

Cimon, when baniſhed by the Oſtraciſm from Athens, joined the army of the Athenians when they were about joining battle with the Lacedemonians, who had always been his friends, and with whom he was accuſed of carrying on a ſecret and traiterous correſpondence. But his enemies of the popular faction procured an order of the council, forbidding him to be preſent at the battle; he retired accordingly, but conjured his friends, who were likewiſe ſuſpected of favouring the enemy, to prove his and their innocence by deeds; and they, placing Cimon's armour in the middle of their little batallion, fought and died in his ſtead for their country.

The oath which every young Athenian was obliged to take, on the completion of his twentieth year, when he was admitted among the number of citizens, was in the following form: " I will never diſgrace myſelf in war; I will never ſeek to ſave my life, by an ignominious flight; I will fight for my country to the laſt drop of my blood, in the ranks of my fellow citizens, or alone if circumſtances require it; I will devote all the days of my

life

life to the fervice of my country; and Agraules, Mars, and Jupiter bear witnefs of my fincerity."

Thrafybulus, who, after the Peloponefian war, delivered his country from the power of the thirty tyrants, animated his fellow-citizens and fellow-foldiers with thefe words : " Let us fight like men, who can only by victory recover our properties, our families, and our country ; let every individual, among us conduct himfelf in fuch a manner as, without prefumption, to think he owes thofe great advantages, together with the honour of victory, to his own arm and his own courage : he that outlives this day, and fees old age ; he that can behold the completion of his renown and his deliverance, will be happy ; but he who fhall be liberated from his bands by death, will be no lefs happy, for no monument is fo glorious as the memorial of having died for one's country."

The Lacedemonians were often unfortunate in their fecond war with the Meffenians : the courage of this warlike people began to fink, and the republic thought itfelf near deftruction. The Delphian oracle propofed the humiliating expedient to the Lacedemonians, to requeft a man from the Athenians to affift them in this dangerous crifis, and who might fupport them by his counfel and talents. Athens fent them, in derifion, the poet Tyrteus:

the

the Lacedemonians, however, received him as the facred meffenger of the divinity; yet they were again defeated three times fucceffively, and prepared to return to Sparta. Tyrteus oppofed this difhonourable determination with all his power, and laboured inceffantly by his fongs, filled with the moft ardent glow of patriotifm, to rekindle the depreffed courage of the Spartan troops; he foon fucceeded in regenerating in every heart the love of its country and the contempt of death; their valour refumed its activity : they attacked the victorious Meffenians with an enthufiaftic prowefs, and were victorious in their turn.

Epaminondas lay ftretched on the ground, and mortally wounded in the breaft by a fpear; but he was only uneafy for the fate of his arms and the event of the battle.   As foon as his fhield was fhewn him, and he was affured that the Thebans had gained the victory, he turned himfelf with a quiet and chearful countenance to the byftanders and faid, " My friends, do not look on this day as the laft of my life, but as the firft of my happinefs and of the completion of my glory; I leave my country victorious, the proud Spartans humbled, and Greece emancipated from fervitude;" then drawing the fteel out of his wound, he expired without a groan.

After

. After the unfortunate battle of Leuctra, the Spartan
mothers, whofe fons had died on the field of battle,
joyfully went to the temple, crowned with garlands
of flowers, to thank the gods for having given them
fuch noble children; while, on the contrary, thofe
mothers whofe fons had faved themfelves by flight,
concealed themfelves in the inmoft receffes of their
houfes, deeply funk in grief, and keeping a death-
like filence; being afhamed to have borne children
who fled from their enemies.

The Spartan matron, who was told the death of
her fon in the fervice of his country, nobly and ftoi-
cally replied, " It was for that end he was born.".

" O traveller, inform the Lacedemonians, that
we lie here, purfuant to the laws of our country,"
was the truly laconic epitaph of thofe who fell at
the battle of Thermopylæ.

For liberty and their country, thofe watch-words
of every people not yet in chains, the Privernates
maintained a long and obftinate war againft the
Romans; they were at length fo weakened, that,
forced to fly on all fides, they were at laft obliged
to fhut themfelves up in their city, which was
befieged and taken by the conful Plautius.   As
this was the fecond revolt of the Privernates
from the dominion of Rome, they were deemed
worthy

worthy of exemplary punifhment; but Plautius,interceded with the fenate for the innocent multitude, and particularly for the prifoners taken in the war, whom he brought to the door of the fenate-houfe; he did not, however, immediately draw the confcript fathers over to his fentiments: they were divided in opinion.   One of the Privernates, by an haughty anfwer, endangered all his fellow-captives. Being afked by a fenator "What punifhment he thought the Privernates deferved?"—"The fame," faid he, "which is due to men, who think themfelves worthy of liberty, and who perfevere in every poffible meafure to preferve it." So daring an anfwer exafperated fome of the affembly; which Plautius perceiving, endeavoured to prevent the ill effects of it, by putting a milder queftion to the prifoner; and which would naturally draw a fofter anfwer from him: "Suppofe," faid the conful, "we fhould grant you pardon and peace; in what manner may we expect you will behave yourfelves for the future?" The prifoner anfwered, "If the conditions of the peace you may impofe on us are juft and humane, and if we need not blufh to have accepted them, we fhall maintain it faithfully and inviolably; but if it be a difgraceful peace, you muft not hope that the neceffity which to-day compels us to fubfcribe to it, will to-morrow oblige us to obferve it." Thefe words made different impreffions upon the judges; fome conftrued

them

them as menaces, and an indication of a difpofition to a new revolt; but the greater and wifer part applauded the magnanimity of the fentiments they expreffed. Thofe efpecially of the fenators, who had filled the curule chair, adhered to the opinion of Plautius, who loudly declared, and repeated it often, " that a people, whofe only defire was liberty, and whofe only fear was that of lofing it; were worthy to be made Roman citizens." Accordingly, the fenate paffed a decree in favour of the prifoners, and Privernum became a Municipium.

Examples of this nature fhine in hiftory as patterns to pofterity. They awaken in every noble mind an irrefragable fenfe of the duties we owe to our country; and the prefervation of the hiftory of thefe examples is nothing more than the propagation of that national pride founded on real advantages.

By the propagation, therefore, of a laudable national pride, the love of its country is introduced into every heart. All breafts are acceffible to this pride, and they are all hurried away by the magic of thefe examples, to the invincible attachment it generates. The continual retrofpect of former times, and the continual contemplation of futurity, are reciprocally the caufes and effects of this pride, and of this love. An honeft patriot will fooner

R   die

die than commit any deed for which his children muft blufh when he is laid in his grave; while nothing feems more noble or fublime to him than the thought that his pofterity will rejoice in his virtues and be refpected on his account.   .

When, therefore, by the revival of thefe fenti-ments the principles and maxims of a nation take a new turn, the actions of its citizens will likewife be ennobled and will rife to the level of their ac-quired fenfations. The man who hopes to attain any poft of honour in the commonwealth, without daring to think on any fubject with manlinefs, freedom, liberality, and penetration, will, inftead of fucceeding in his views, be an object of derifion and contempt. Integrity will ever keep in mind the public welfare, and contribute its utmoft to the pro-motion of it, notwithftanding mean and little minds · may call it improvidence and indifcretion, whofe views are directed wholly towards the benefit of their families. Inequality of condition will lofe its vexatious nature, when there exifts but one politi-cal virtue, and when all are united under the noble appellation of citizen. The attachment to their country will no longer depend merely upon the un-certainty of greater happinefs in another; for many will willingly live content with the bare neceffaries, rather than quit their country in purfuit of the luxu-ries of other climes. Every one will obey his fuperior

more

more from inclination than duty, more from affection than obligation. The government will no
more be the foul of many bodies, but rather the
foul of one body.

Thefe advantages will be more difcernible when
I confider them in another point of view, and prove
how very impatient the cultivation of a noble pride
is to a nation palfied by the decay of its virtue.

The noble pride of a nation is diminifhed or an-
nihilated when the advantages gained by the virtues
of their fathers are loft through the vices of their
defcendants. Times are altered, is a common faying, and the conclufion to be formed from it is
neither difficult nor fubtle. Times, to be fure,
would be much altered, with regard to a nation
who depended on mufcular ftrength of body, if
they were to be collected to fight but one battle
now the art of flaughter is brought to fuch perfection; yet no one doubts the indifpenfable
neceffity of the modern art of war. But it is not
only the knowledge of the management of arms
that is neceffary to a free-born nation; it muft
likewife have an intellectual knowledge, and be
endowed with principles and fentiments, and thefe
are not inftilled by the blows of a cane or the
found of a drum.

In.

In this refpect, the change of times makes the refumption of ancient maxims but too needful. Though courage and zeal in the fervice of the ftate are very often out of fafhion, yet they are never ufelefs, always denoting vigour. When, therefore, a nation feems to lofe its fpirit, becaufe its foil is no more dyed with the blood of its fons; when the noble flame, formerly kindled by the love of liberty, is fmothered by an almoft univerfal lethargy; when indolence is chofen for the laft intrenchment; when nurfed in luxury and terror, the mind lofes the whole of its pith and ftrength; when enormous expences make avarice and the thirft of gold a neceffary evil; when cowardice raifes into confideration, and valour depreffes into misfortune; when men, not thinking they ftand any more in need of prowefs, fall into every kind of profligacy; when even the crimes which require a certain ftrength and elevation of mind are not to be met with; when felfifhnefs is no more thought a vice, and the timid prudence of a moment no more a fault in politics; when ambition, inftead of endeavouring to excel its rivals, feeks only to blacken them by calumny: then, I fay, the revival of national pride would be a meafure of no little efficacy to rekindle the fire of ancient virtue, and reproduce the powers of youth and manhood in the decay of age, when the nation feems to be near the laft ftruggles of diffolution.

All

All expectation of the revival of a noble pride, however, feems to be vain, when, in a free nation, there are too many people in whofe eyes Phocion was a fool; too many who look down upon a hero with a haughty pity; who do not believe that there ever exifted any great men; who think fame an empty bubble, becaufe it has always proved impoffible for them to do any thing worthy of it; who contract their brows into the appearance of a frown, which vifibly betrays their timorous emotions, when the word freedom is pronounced by an adventurous innovator in their prefence; who would exclude from the prefs the moft fublime monuments of the honour of their formerly fimple and unfophifticated nation, in which the heroic deeds of their fathers are depicted in the moft lively colours, by which the love of virtue, of concord, of liberty, of religion, of their country, and of the laws would, like a ftream of fire, rufh into every heart, and awaken in it at the fame time an utter averfion to the poifon of foreign manners, to prodigality, to effeminancy, and to avarice; adducing in their fupport, this fhameful and pitiful maxim, " That it is dangerous to pull down an old houfe over your fhoulders."

Thomas Abbt, a man of real genius, whom I cannot name without expreffing my reverence for his memory, fays very pertinently, that the exam-

ples

ples of patriots appear with fuch luftre in the annals of republics, fince it is their intereft to procure the rewards due to their greateft worthies from pofterity, becaufe their contemporaries were too poor to afford them.   The duties of remembrance, of gratitude, and of emulation, are, therefore, impofed on us with refpeḉt to our anceftors, and we can never fulfil thefe, if we look with indifference on what is great and good in their manners and aḉtions; if we turn away our eyes in difguft from their contemplation, without deigning to be proud of them. It was only the memory of their great men, that preferved among the Greeks, the thirft of honour, difintereftednefs, and devotion to the public good.

The fate of this fo neceffary national pride depends upon that of the love of one's country. There are many accidental occurrences by which this laft is fometimes carried to a genial warmth, whence the ftate receives the moft excellent fruits; fometimes to an immoderate heat, which entirely parches it up; fometimes, in a people no longer fufceptible of the love of liberty, it will be fo much refrigerated that its fruits cannot ripen.   The chilling hand of death ftretched its baleful influence over the liberty of the Athenians, when, in the days of their lethargy and weaknefs, they erected altars to the honour of the harlots of Demetrius, and decreed, by a public ediḉt, that all the commands of

king

king Demetrius fhould at Athens, be held facred
before the gods, and juft before men.

But emergencies fometimes arife, when the man
who thought to plough his field in quietnefs and
eafe, muft grafp a fword inftead of his inftruments
of hufbandry; when we are no more to confine
our thoughts and cares to what regards ourfelves;
when bullies, coxcombs, and idlers are called to
other bufinefs, than to loiter about from one company of females to another, boafting of their
amours, their inconftancies, and their idle
purfuits; when thofe, who know only how to
command, muft learn to obey; when it is not
thought a misfortune to have fellow-citizens of
genius and talents; when we wifh to hear the
words liberty and my country repeated with ardour by every mouth; when thofe are no more
declaimed againft as ridiculous enthufiafts who,
in callous times, have inceffantly reminded their
nation of its priftine glory, of the time when its
inhabitants were poor, virtuous, bold, and free;
when fields were cultivated by the victorious hands
of the defenders of their country, and their ploughfhares encircled with laurels. There are times, I fay,
when thofe, whom nature has gifted with energy
and elevation of foul, and minds capable of the
fublimeft virtues, are no longer watched as fufpected and dangerous fubjects; when thofe who,

in the career of youth, for want of the apprehen-
fions and timidity, mifcalled moderation and prudence, which are too often the confequence of
experience, and have perhaps been impelled by
an ardent principle of patriotic virtue beyond the
bounds of real prudence; who have awakened the
fear of their fellow-citizens, when they thought
they beheld impending or diftant dangers threaten
their country; and who have wanted only an occafion to fhed their willing blood in its behalf; are
efteemed truly patriots; when the empty applaufe
of a few titled fools will not be procured at the
expence of turning into ridicule the noble enthufiafm and virtuous principles of a whole nation;
when hofts of foreign enemies affail it on all fides,
whofe attack feems to threaten inevitable ruin.

A nation will therefore never lofe its honour
as long as its virtue remains unpolluted, and its
virtue will never be tainted, as long as patriotifm
gives a free and lofty flight to every fentiment of
the heart.

Finally, national pride, founded on real advantages, has likewife its defective fide. A celebrated northern philofopher has made this important remark, verified by daily experience, " That
there are never any laudable fentiments, any glorious
talents or faculties in human nature, which do not

at

at the fame time, by infinite gradation, degenerate into the very oppofite imperfections." Hence, it is evident, that the extremes of reafonable and ridiculous pride often naturally run into each other.

The defects of great minds flow from their pride, when this degenerates into vanity. Dazzled by the flattery of their admirers, thefe demi-gods fhut their ears as much to truth as the weakeft princes; intoxicated with the fenfe of their real advantages, they do not comprehend that thefe are not every where current for them. Whoever always feeks applaufe, will always be liable to meet with mortification in the extreme, and, in fact, will feldom efcape it. He will, at laft, nearly look upon himfelf as the only being of confequence in the world, and all its other inhabitants either as his admirers or his enviers; but one of the ancients fays exceedingly well: "If thou wilt not be juft and righteous without the oftentation of thy juftice and righteoufnefs, thou wilt often be fo with fhame and derifion." The fecret of the moft fubtle vanity is, on the other hand, nothing elfe than the art of making one's felf prized, without either appearing to be vain or felf-conceited. Cicero was ignorant of this art, or he would not have attracted the hatred of the Romans as he did, by the everrecurring praife of himfelf and his actions; it was the text of all his orations, and never failed to offend

offend his hearers, becaufe he feemed to efteem his fervices every thing, and thofe of other men as nothing.

Pride is always mifplaced when it cannot command refpect. It is very evident, that a man who is conftantly and habitually proud, cannot poffibly be fo, on account of real advantages, fince he difgufts all mankind by his pride, makes himfelf defpicable and ridiculous in every refpect, and blinks through the fpectacles of felf-conceit, until all around him are exafperated to hatred and to goading farcafm; and the contempt which is thus returned is generally much ftronger than that occafioning it. Aftonifhed at his fuperiority over the reft of the world, fuch a man endeavours to imprefs others with the fame refpect he entertains for himfelf, and of which he is fo full; he accuftoms himfelf to awe freeborn men beneath his frowns, in the perfons of his grooms and footmen; he thinks that all beneath him, all on a level with him, nay his acknowledged fuperiors, may be called the populace; but an author, the beft acquainted with man, the comic writer Sterne, fays, " In fober truth, 'tis but a fcurvy kind of a trick, (quoties voluit fortuna jocari,) when fortune, in one of her merry moods, takes a poor devil, with this paffion in his head, and mounts him up at once as high as fhe can get him, for it is fure to make him play fuch fantaftic

2   tricks

tricks as to become the very fool of the comedy;
and was he not a general benefactor to mankind
in making it merry, I know not how fpleen could
be pacified during the reprefentation."

Nothing upon earth is perfect; virtue even has
its vulnerable points, the fun its fpots, and a con-
fcientious prude, who has paffed the ordeal of grace,
may fall. We muft not always judge of men
who are thought great, by their writings or their
words, we muft alfo view their every action; we
muft ftudy them in their lives, in their families,
and in their houfes, if we would rightly know them.
The old and rigid Cato had a concubine as well as
the philofophical emperor Marcus Antoninus, and
many a modern philofopher whom I know. The
greateft men are always connected with the reft of
mankind by fome foible or other; and yet there
are few of them who are fo candid as Antigonus,
who, on Hermodotus faluting him as a deity and
the child of the fun, told him very judicioufly
" to afk the fervant who emptied his clofe-ftool his
opinion upon this fubject."

The greateft talents affume a hateful appearance,
when they are accompanied by arrogance or break
out in contempt of others. Contempt in an arrogant man confifts in the affection with which he
fhews, without referve, his fenfe of the real or
imaginary

imaginary inferiority of another. Contempt in a proud man confifts in the fenfe of the real inferiority of another, which he expofes when it ought to be expofed, and conceals where it ought to be concealed. This fenfe is infeparable from the nobleft minds, and is ever juft in itfelf, for it is impoffible that any one can miftake a cat for an elephant, or a gnat for a mountain, but it is exceedingly offenfive when it difcovers defects where they ought not to be obferved.

A well-founded and noble felf-efteem degenerates fometimes into temerity and prefumption. Fanaticifm is called a devout prefumption, which by an excefs of pride and felf-confidence left to itfelf, pretends to approach the divine nature, and to exalt itfelf by an aftonifhing flight above the ufual and prefcribed order of things. It is greatly to be regretted, that fometimes the moral writers, as they are called, abandon themfelves to this giddy prefumption, when they do not fufficiently weigh againft each other our duties and our means of difcharging them ; when, in their reveries, they do not recollect that they defire impoffibilities, and that they rob virtue of its charms, by fubftituting their rhapfodies and chimæras in the place of virtue, while they endeavour to deceive the public into an acquiefcence with their eccentric ideas.

The

The well-founded pride of whole nations, like-wife, has its blind fide. No nation can be with juftice unboundedly proud; great virtues are accompanied with great faults, every good with its attendant evils, and every advantage with its inconveniences. It is no crime to expofe this fact to a nation with rational fincerity. My dear friend, Mr. Ifelin, who well deferves attention, fays, in the preface to his beautiful but very fhort Hiftory of Helvetian Virtue, " That every nation fhould promife a reward to thofe who fhall difplay, in the moft obvious light, the defects of its conftitution and manners, and the vices and faults of its progenitors, as well as their virtues."

People are often alfo proud of advantages, which, though real, they do not owe to themfelves. The warmth or temperatenefs of a climate, the denfity or rarefaction of the air, the nature of the foil, of the water and the winds, together with the manner of living, and the cuftoms, have all fuch a vifible influence upon the faculties of whole nations, that they ought not to afcribe them folely to their own individual exertions. A worthy man may be proud of his virtues, for they are his own, but why fhould we pride ourfelves upon our underftanding, when the fineft intellects are liable to be deranged by the moft trivial phyfical accidents. Independant of external circumftances; a little extraneous air in the

bowels,

bowels, or an indigeftible lump in the ftomach, and lo, the divine light of the foul is extinguifhed!

We but too feldom calculate how little of our own honour really belongs to ourfelves. There are few men fo honeft as Antiochus Soter, who wept for fpite on account of his victory over the Gala-tians, conceiving that he was not indebted, for it to his own prowefs or conduct, but to the dreadful havoc made by his elephants, and he, for that rea-fon, caufed trophies to be erected on the field of battle, not dedicated to himfelf, but to thefe power-ful four-footed auxiliaries.

Yet there are many deteftable vices which arife from a national pride not altogether ignoble. The Canadian favage is extremely proud; he feels the full worth of freedom, and is impatient of control, even in his infancy; reftlefs under the leaft con-ftraint of education, he refufes to fubmit even to parental authority; but a generous forgivenefs of offences is wholly unknown to him as a virtue; he defpifes it as a miferable weaknefs: intrepidity is his greateft merit, and the enjoyment of revenge his fweeteft luxury.

The love of our country, too, requires fometimes a curb as well as a fpur. It has been very fhrewdly remarked, that the law-givers of ancient republics
have

have fought more eagerly to infpire the people with this noble fentiment, and to extend and ftrengthen it in their hearts, than to fet the bounds which reafon prefcribes fo as to render them perceptible to the multitude, and to make them comprehend why it is neceffary that the love of their country ought to be circumfcribed and governed by reafon.

In their moft exalted days, the Greeks held the love of their country as the firft civil virtue. We certainly owe a higher degree of that affection we ought to bear towards all mankind, to our parents, our wives, and our children, than to ftrangers ; and a greater meafure of the good will, which human nature in general requires at our hands, to our own country, which is the proper feat of our activity, the ftation appointed to us by Providence for the exercife of every focial duty. But this limitation, this contraction of our philanthropy, often makes us narrow-minded, felfifh, and unjuft, nay, fometimes iniquitoufly barbarous towards all other nations. As the love of mankind, like that of beauty, feldom can be made to attach fo forcibly to the abfent, as to thofe who are prefent, fo we always efteem the Europeans more than the Africans, the Afiatics, or the Americans, our own countrymen more than foreigners, and our fellow-citizens more than our fellow-fubjects ; but by thus gradually receding from univerfal philanthropy, we are infenfibly led

to

to hate all that is not immediately connected with us by the bands of interest or confanguinity, and fometimes even fnap thefe afunder : a convincing proof of a mifanthropic difpofition not unfrequent in human nature. I know an European city, the government whereof poffeffes an extenfive and beautiful tract of land, which is happy under its fway ; but, unfortunately, the exclufive predilect-ion in favour of their fellow-citizens is fo violent a paffion in all the weak heads of this city, that they deprive the inhabitants of all the towns in their territory of emulation, excluding them from the enjoyment of all rewards or marks of honour, and in the fits of their madnefs, would willingly drown them all, if it was in their power.

The more we cleave to the particular and indi-vidual intereft of our own country, the lefs philan-thropic we moft affuredly become.   Such patriots act in general moft repugnantly towards foreigners, becaufe they are fo, and of courfe are nothing in their eftimation.   The Jews of the old teftament, were fo much attached to their country, that they neglected the duties of humanity towards ftrangers. The Greeks defpifed all foreigners as barbarians, and thought them deftined to be their flaves, be-caufe nature had given them lefs genius and under-ftanding.   The virtuous Spartans were unjuft and fraudulent towards ftrangers.   A Japanefe, who
fhould

fhould chance to fhew the leaft efteem or friendfhip for a Dutchman, would be pointed at as an enemy of his country, fince he was not attached to it in exclufion of the reft of mankind. They think it contrary to the interefts of Japan, to the commands of the emperor, to the will of the gods, and to the dictates of their confcience, to feel the leaft inclination towards a foreigner. This is in general the policy that may be faid to actuate the mercantile powers of Europe, who, confidered in this point of view, feem wholly to be animated with the meaneft felf-love; for they not only overlook the depredations of the piratical ftates of Barbary upon the fubjects and property of thofe nations, who, both by every principle of religion and policy are the eternal enemies of the crefcent, but even form difgraceful alliances with thefe freebooters, and fubmit to the groffeft affronts and injuries from them, feeming even to authorife what humanity fhudders to think of, for the fake of the pitiful advantage arifing from the monopoly of the trade of the Mediterranean.

But in our times, we have lefs to fear the evil effects of patriotifm. I am acquainted with men who are anxious to promote both the general and particular welfare of their country, and afpire to this laudable purfuit at every ftep; who divide their duties into tafks, and perform firft thofe which are the moft univerfally benevolent, and produce the moft gene-

s   ral

ral good to their country; whofe courage is not daunted when their friends weakly abandon them, either from the bare view of the power of their antagonifts, or of the menacing authoritative frowns of the flanderers of their principles; who depart not for a moment, from the line of their duties, either from interefted or erroneous motives; who feel that their fouls are like lambent flames, which, tending in their own effence upwards, can never fink to the bottom; whom no refufal can intimidate, no oppofition drive from their ftedfaft and noble purpofe; who never draw back; in whom the love of eafe never renders the rational, but too often ufelefs combat, againft the ignorance and depravity of mankind, a burden; who, in a word, love their country with a filial affection, forgive its injuries, and excufe its errors, and would rather endure death, in a thoufand fhapes, than once give room to think, that their zeal for their country would ever abate on account of the difregard it may fhew to their perfonal merit. But the number of anti-patriots feems in our days to have increafed, and much more fo, that of the hypocrites, who boaft of their oaths and deareft duties, folely becaufe thefe are fometimes the only paths to honours, dignity, and riches; while avarice and felf-intereft are the fole motives of all their actions. Many a one exclaims that he loves his country, who loves nothing but himfelf; many a one thunders forth his patriotifm on all
public

public occafions, while the cunning villain fecretly
ftretches out his itching palm to receive his yearly,
wages in foreign gold. When here and there
the torch of patriotifm is uplifted, the fparks generally fall on the fingers of the patriots, and this
fentiment feems fometimes to actuate every breaft,
while it is, in fact, only the fafhionable whim of
the day ; and our young fellows now travel to become patriots, as they formerly did to become
orators and cognofcenti.

Well-founded national pride has thus both confiderable advantages, as well as evils proceeding
from thefe very advantages. Virtues and vices are
often called into action by the fame motives ; it is
the tafk of the philofopher to difcover thefe motives,
and that of the legiflator to make a proper ufe of
the difcovery.

Pride is therefore the fource of fo many
beneficial talents, and of fo many virtues, that we
ought not to endeavour to deftroy it, but to make
it fubfervient to good purpofes. Man would be a
fenfelefs block, if he were forbidden every thing
that could lead him aftray. We muft inevitably
banifh good fenfe from a whole nation, if, more
attentive to particular than to general imperfections,
we were to attempt to command fentiments, rather
than to infpire them ; and we fhould act againft

our

our own feelings, if, inftead of adapting faults to the good of the whole, inftead of conducting mankind by their paffions, and of employing their foibles, even to lead them to good, we were to fmother principles and fentiments, which are able to animate a whole nation, and to excite it to the nobleft actions.

F I N I S.

INDEX.

A

Arabians,

INDEX.

Benedict

s 4   *Carnival,*

INDEX.

Chinefe

I N D E X.

Galeas,

INDEX.

G

H

I—J

Japaneſe,

INDEX.

Morocco,

Nile,

Perſian

I N · D · E · X.

Spaniards,

Terrubia's

INDEX.

INDEX.

BOOKS

Printed for and Sold by C. DILLY, POULTRY, LONDON.

---

1. SOLITUDE confidered, with refpect to its Influence upon the Mind and the Heart. By Dr. Zimmermann. 8vo. 7s.

2. Falconer's Differtation on the Influence of the Paffions upon the Diforders of the Body. Third edition, 2s. 6d. boards.

3. Anarchafis (Voyage du Jeune) en Grèce, dans le milieu du quatrième fiècle, avant l'ère vulgaire. 3 tom. 8vo. avec cartes, plans, &c. 1l. 7s.

4. Ditto, elegantly printed upon a fuperfine wove royal paper, the Maps, &c. coloured, 1l. 16s. boards.

5. Bath Society's Papers on Agriculture, Planting, &c. 8 vols. 2l. 5s.

6. Bofwell's Life of Dr. Johnfon, 3 vols. 8vo. fecond edition, 1l. 7s.

7. Bofwell's Journal of a Tour to the Hebrides, with S. Johnfon, LL. D. with a Map, defcribing the Track of the Travellers. 8vo. 7s.

8. Bowdler's (Mifs) Poems and Effays, fmall 8vo. 6s.

9. Bowles's (Rev. W. L.) Sonnets, and other Poems, fourth edition, 4s. fewed.

10. Britifh Plutarch; containing the Lives of the moft eminent Statefmen, Patiots, Divines, Warriors, Philofophers, Poets, and Artifts, of Great Britain and Ireland, from the Acceffion of Henry VIII. to the prefent Time. Including a compendious View of the Hiftory of England during that Period, 8 vols. 12mo. 1l. 4s.

11. Burgh's Dignity of Human Nature; or a brief Account of the certain and eſtabliſhed Means for attaining the true End of our Exiſtence. A New Edition, to which is prefixed, Some Account of the Author. 8vo. 7. 6d.

12. Brown's Eſſay on the Natural Equality of Men; on the Rights that reſult from it, and on the Duties which it impoſes, crown 8vo. 5s.

13. Camper (Profeſſor) on the Connection between Anatomy and the Arts of Drawing, Painting, Statuary, &c. Tranſlated by Dr. Cogan, 4to. with Plates, by Kirk, 1l. 1s. boards.

14. Catechiſm of Health, for Domeſtic Inſtruction; tranſlated from the German of Dr. Fauſt, 12mo. 2s. ſewed. Ditto, fine paper, boards, 2s. 6d.

15. Cheſterfield's (Lord) Miſcellaneous Works; conſiſting of Letters to his Friends, never before printed, and various other articles. To which are prefixed, Memoirs of his Life, tending to illuſtrate the civil, literary, and political Hiſtory of his Time; by M. Maty, 2 vols. royal 4to. 2l. 8s.

16. Etudes de la Nature, par Jaques Henri-Barnardin de Saint Pierre, 2 tom. 8vo.

17. Ditto, Printed on a ſuperfine wove medium paper.

18. Fothergill's (Dr.) Works, with the Life of the Author, by Dr. Lettſom, 3 vols. 8vo. 1l. 1s.

19. Ditto, 4to. 1l. 16s.

20. Fothergill's Life and Tracts, ſeparate, 8vo. 7s.

21. Franklin's (Dr. Benj.) Philoſophical and Miſcellaneous Papers, never before collected, 8vo. 3s. 6d. ſewed.

22. Franklin on Smokey Chimnies, ſeparate, 2s.

23. Guthrie's New Syſtem of Modern Geography, 4to. the Maps half-bound, ſeparate, 2l. 6s.

24. The ſame on a fine Royal Paper, 2l. 12s. 6d. in boards.

25. Howard's State of Priſons in England and Wales, new edition, 4to. 1l. 5s.

26. Howard's Account of the principal Lazarettos in Europe, 4to. new edition, 1l. 5s.

27. Howard's Appendix to ditto, 4to. ftiched, 2s. 6d.

28. Holwell's (The Rev. William, B. D.) Mythological, Etymological, and Hiftorical Dictonary, 8vo. 7s.

29. Dr. Johnfon's Works, 12 vol. 8vo. new edition, with Additions; and an Effay on his Life and Genius, by Murphy, 4l. 4s.

30. Jones's (Sir William) Speeches of Ifæus, 10s. 6d. boards.

31. Jones's Mahomedan Law, 5s.

32. Knox's Sermons, chiefly intended to promote Faith, Hope, and Charity, 8vo. 7s.

33. Knox's Effays, Moral and Literary, on a large Letter, 3 vols. 8vo. 1l. 1s.

34. Another edition. 2 vols. 12mo. 8s.

35. Knox on a Liberal Education, 2 vols. 12mo. 8s.

36. Knox's Winter Evenings, 2 vols. 12mo. 8s.

37. Knox's Elegant Extracts; or Ufeful and Entertaining Paffages in Profe ; felected for the Improvement of Scholars at Claffical and other Schools in the Art of Speaking, in Reading, Thinking, Compofing ; and in the Conduct of Life, large 8vo. 14s.

38. Knox's Elegant Extracts in Poetry, felected from various Englifh Authors; being fimilar in Defign to the Profe Extracts, large 8vo. 16s.

39. Knox's Elegant Epiftles : or, A Copious Collection of Familiar and Amufing Letters, felected for the Improvement of Young Perfons, and for general Entertainment, large 8vo. 12s.

40 Knox's Chriftian Philofophy ; or an attempt to Difplay the Evidence and Excellence of Revealed Religion, 12mo. 6s.

41. Milton's Paradife Loft, elegantly printed by Mr. Benfley, on a fuperfine wove paper, fmall 8vo. ornamented with an Emblematical Frontifpiece, and two Vignettes, defigned by Burney, and Engraved by Heath, &c. 10s.6d.

42. Milton's Paradife Regained, and other Poems, printed uniformly with the above, with three elegant Engravings from Defigns by Burney, 10s. 6d.

43. Playfair's (Dr.) Syftem of Chronology, elegantly printed on a new Great Primer Type, and a fine Royal Paper, in one large volume, folio, 2l. 12s. 6d.

44. Pope's Homer's Iliad and Odyffey, with notes by Wakefield, 11 vols. 8vo. 4l. 8s.

45. Ruffel's (Lady Rachael) Letters, a new edition, ornamented with an Hiftorical Engraving, and Portraits of Lord and Lady Ruffel, 8vo. 10s.

46. Studies of Nature, tranflated from the French of James Henry Bernardin de Saint Pierre, by Henry Hunter, D. D. 5 vols. 8vo. embellifhed with five Explanatory Engravings, 1l. 15s.

47. The fame printed on a fine Wove Royal Paper, 2l. 2s. in boards.

48. Towers's Memoirs of the Life and Reign of Frederick the Third, King of Pruffia, 2 vols. 8vo. fecond edition, 16s.

49. Townfend's Journey through Spain in 1786 and 1787: with particular Attention to the Agriculture, Manufactures, Commerce, Population, Taxes, and Revenue of that Country; and Remarks on paffing through a part of France, 3 vols. 8vo. 18s.

50. Tracks of Warburton and a Warburtonian, not admitted into the Collection of their refpective Works, with Prefaces, by Dr. Parr. 5s. boards.

51.–Tranfactions of the American Philofophical Society, held at Philadelphia, for promoting ufeful Knowledge. 3 vols. 4to. 2l. 14s. boards.

52. Wraxall's Tour through the Weftern, Southern, and Interior Provinces of France, 12mo. 3s.

53. Wraxall's Hiftory of the Kings of France, of the Houfe of Valois, 2 vols. 8vo. 12s.

www.ingramcontent.com/pod-product-compliance
Lightning Source LLC
Chambersburg PA
CBHW060515030726
47498CB00004B/949